WHERE WOMEN COOK
CELEBRATE!
EXTRAORDINARY WOMEN & THEIR SIGNATURE RECIPES

by Jo Packham & The Publishers of Somerset Studio

LARK

An Imprint of Sterling Publishing Co., Inc.
New York

WWW.LARKCRAFTS.COM

Cover Design & Art Director:

Matt Shay

Library of Congress Cataloging-in-Publication Data

Packham, Jo.
 Where women cook: celebrate! extraordinary women &
their signature recipes / Jo Packham. -- 1st ed.
    p. cm.
 Includes index.
 ISBN 978-1-60059-898-2 (hc-cloth : alk. paper)
 1. Entertaining. 2. Cooking. 3. Cooks. I. Title.
 TX731.P24 2011
 642'.4--dc22

                                            2010051967

10 9 8 7 6 5 4 3 2 1

First Edition

Published by Lark Crafts
An Imprint of Sterling Publishing Co., Inc.
387 Park Avenue South, New York, NY 10016

Text © 2011, Jo Packham
Photography © 2011, Lark Crafts, an Imprint of Sterling
Publishing Co., Inc., unless otherwise specified

Distributed in Canada by Sterling Publishing,
c/o Canadian Manda Group, 165 Dufferin Street
Toronto, Ontario, Canada M6K 3H6

Distributed in the United Kingdom by GMC Distribution Services,
Castle Place, 166 High Street, Lewes, East Sussex, England BN7 1XU

Distributed in Australia by Capricorn Link (Australia) Pty Ltd.,
P.O. Box 704, Windsor, NSW 2756 Australia

If you have questions or comments about this book, please contact:
Lark Crafts
67 Broadway
Asheville, NC 28801
828-253-0467

Manufactured in China

ISBN 13: 978-1-60059-898-2

For information about custom editions, special sales, premium
and corporate purchases, please contact Sterling Special Sales
Department at 800-805-5489 or specialsales@sterlingpub.com.

For information about desk and examination copies available to college and
university professors, requests must be submitted to academic@larkbooks.
com. Our complete policy can be found at www.larkcrafts.com.

Foreword

Celebrations … what are they really?

Does a celebration require formal attire, linen tablecloths, massive bouquets of fresh flowers, and fine wine—or will a picnic table and a packed lunch do the trick? Should the food and mood be extravagant? Must a room be filled with people to feel merry? Or can a few special souls make an event memorable for the host? Do you need a reason or an excuse to plan a party, or is no reason at all save the everyday joys of family or friendship all the inspiration you need? Does your gathering have to mark a certain day? Do you follow revered traditions or embark on new adventures in entertaining?

To any one of these questions, you might answer "yes," "sometimes," "maybe," or "not always." An ordinary fall day with colors so bright they light the autumn air can be enough of a reason to celebrate. It might be just the two of you sharing an occasion, or you might want to invite all the people you know to celebrate with you. And then there are those very important moments we celebrate all by ourselves.

The food that is served seems to be the main component of any celebration, on any day, for any reason, for any number of people. After all, there must be drinks with which to toast, appetizers to begin conversations by, main courses (the sight of which may make your mouth water) to savor together, and those desserts that have become the accepted definition of well-earned, albeit guilty, pleasures.

Here on the pages of **WHERE WOMEN COOK CELEBRATE!** are the stories, the food, the reasons, and the celebrated times of extraordinary women. These gatherings, as varied as the women hosting them, are the reminder that each of us has so very much to celebrate . . . even on an ordinary spring day in April.

Read their stories, make their food, enjoy their parties … it will bring you such joy!

Jo Packham

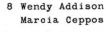

ingredients

A HALLOWEEN CIRCUS MASQUERADE

At Tinsel Trading Company

Wendy Addison & Marcia Ceppos

When Wendy Addison of the Theatre of Dreams and Marcia Ceppos of Tinsel Trading join forces to throw a party, you can bet that there will be more than just great food! Wendy, who works closely with Tinsel Trading as a designer, had a field day with this project by staging the traditional Halloween party at the legendary store in Manhattan.

For ten years, friends, customers, and employees of Tinsel Trading in New York City have gone all out making their own costumes. This year, food and treats were designed around a circus theme, and Wendy Addison supplied a plethora of table decorations to set the mood. Crepe paper banners were hoisted to the ceiling, and an antique linen theatre curtain was hung with a glittered crescent moon for the perfect backdrop for vintage-style party pics.

As guests entered the door, they were greeted by a carnival strongman, Robert Warner, complete with handlebar mustache, offering muslin bags of freshly roasted peanuts and popcorn. Carolina, who strolled the gathering with a tray of Cracker Jack, also wears one of the circus hats provided. Palms were read by Madame Zuba (Jennifer) in her fortune telling booth, as calliope music wafted through the air!

The ringmaster cracked her whip, the strongman hoisted a trapeze artiste, and the circus lion roared with excitement!

The refreshments were consumed, and the entire party posed in their fabulous costumes for a keepsake picture. After the last cupcake disappeared and the peanut shells were swept from the floor, the party was over ... with just the tinkling of the calliope to remember a wonderful day ... at the circus!

Roasted Corn

Serves 12

12 ears of corn, husks removed, rinsed
½ cup (1 stick) unsalted butter, melted
     Good-quality chili powder
1 cup finely chopped fresh cilantro
2 limes, cut in half

1. Place the ears of corn in boiling water and cook for 8 to 10 minutes. Remove and drain. Coat each ear of corn with melted butter.

2. Place the ears of corn over a hot grill, or under a broiler, and cook until the kernels begin to brown. Remove from heat. Add a little more butter, sprinkle lightly with chili powder and chipped cilantro, and follow with a generous squeeze of lime juice. Serve immediately.

Grilled Sausages with Mango Salsa

Serves 12

1 or 2 ripe mangoes
1 large white onion
1 large ripe tomato
1 or 2 ripe avocados
4 to 8 fresh jalapeños, finely minced
6 cloves garlic, finely minced
3 fresh limes, juiced
12 sausages
12 crusty bakery rolls

1. Chop mangoes, onion, tomato, and avocados and mix together in a deep bowl. Add jalapeños, garlic, and lime juice. Let salsa rest at least 1 hour before serving.

2. Grill sausages over an open flame, or under a broiler, until they are nicely browned, 8 to 10 minutes per side. Place each sausage inside a bakery roll and serve with salsa.

"Hold on **tightly**, let go **lightly**."
— The Croupier

Lemon Meringue Cupcakes

Makes 24 cupcakes

- 1 cup (2 sticks) butter, at room temperature
- 2 cups sugar
- 3 extra-large eggs
  Grated zest of 3 or 4 medium-sized lemons
- 2 lemons, juiced
- 1½ tsp. pure vanilla extract
- 3½ cups all-purpose flour
- 1 tsp. baking soda
- ½ tsp. baking powder
- ½ tsp. salt
- 2 cups sour cream

Lemon Curd:

- ¾ cup fresh lemon juice
- 1 TB. grated lemon zest
- ¾ cup sugar
- 3 eggs
- ½ cup unsalted butter, cubed

Meringue Frosting:

- 8 large egg whites
- 2 cups sugar
- ½ tsp. cream of tartar
- 2 tsp. pure vanilla extract

1. Preheat the oven to 350°F. Line muffin tins with 24 paper cups.

2. In an electric mixer, combine butter and sugar. Add eggs, one at a time, and mix until combined. Add zest, lemon juice, and vanilla extract.

3. In a separate bowl, combine flour, baking soda, baking powder, and salt. Add dry ingredients to the butter mixture in thirds, alternating with the sour cream, until evenly combined. Fill each muffin cup two thirds full with batter. Bake for 25 to 30 minutes, or until a toothpick inserted near the center comes out clean. Cool completely on wire racks.

4. Whisk together the lemon juice, zest, sugar and eggs until well combined. Add butter and cook over medium-low heat for 5 to 6 minutes, stirring constantly until the custard is thick enough to coat the back of a spoon.

5. Fill a different medium saucepan halfway with water and bring to a light simmer. In a heatproof bowl of an electric mixer, combine egg whites, sugar, and cream of tartar. Set the mixture over the saucepan and whisk for 3 to 4 minutes, until sugar is dissolved. Transfer bowl to electric mixer and beat for 5 to 6 minutes, or until stiff peaks form. Mix in vanilla and use meringue immediately.

6. Assemble when cupcakes are completely cooled. Spread each cupcake with a thin layer of lemon curd. Finish each one off with a heap of the fresh meringue, making sure to end with a flourish! To brown the tops of the meringue, use a chef's blowtorch or place the cupcakes briefly under a very hot broiler.

A TREAT

HARLEQUIN PARADES!
HALLS OF
HONEYCOMBS
FAIRY BOWERS
STAR SPANGLED DOMES,
AND GLITTERING
SHOWERS!

LUSIONS OF

KITCHEN TABLE TEA

Susan Branch

TEA?

YUM

Susan Branch is the author and artist of twelve charming, whimsical, handwritten and water-colored *Heart of the Home* books. Most of her books are cookbooks, with titles such as *Summer*, *Autumn*, and *Vineyard Seasons*. Susan's art has adorned everything from jammies and dishes to calendars, stationery, and things for scrapbooking, and she designs two quilting fabric collections each year. She blogs on her website *www.susanbranch.com* and sends out a monthly newsletter, "Willard" (named for her grandfather), filled with recipes, craft ideas, quotes, and "stories from home." Susan is a girlfriend's girlfriend, as many of you who are familiar with her book *Girlfriends Forever* know. She invited us into her nineteenth-century home on the island of Martha's Vineyard as she was preparing for what she called "a kitchen table tea."

WHEN TWO FOND HEARTS
AS ONE UNITE
THE YOKE IS EASY
AND THE BURDEN LIGHT

How to go to a Tea Party

By Kitt Macy, Age 9

1. Wear a sutibul dress or skirt never pants or shorts.
2. Don't you ever go on Tuesdays or Friday the 13th.
3. Sip slowly, don't slurp.
4. Be jolly, laugh and eat at least 1 cookie.
5. Make an instring conversation.
6. Thank the host or hostist.
7. Give them at least 1 $.
8. After 5 times in a row the 6th time give a preasent.
9. Go again at least once.
10. Don't go and get things the host will bring it to you.
11. Have a great time!

"In the dell in our garden
My dolls and I take tea,
And days when I have raisins
The catbirds dine with me"

Elisabeth Merrill

"It's not a high tea," Susan explains, "which could have a dozen different little taste treats; this is more of an everyday kind of tea party around the kitchen table, because the focus is on the girlfriends and the talk; a little respite in our day; a chance to catch up. But I still want them to feel special; I use my favorite cups-with-saucers, brew a big pot of lavender Earl Grey tea with honey and cream, and fix some delicious little things to eat. Time out with the girls is good for the soul. My girlfriends know that T-E-A is spelled L-O-V-E."

15

The best aromatherapy comes from the kitchen

Susan's story is inspirational. Her books are embellished with vignettes of her growing up as the oldest of eight children in Southern California. Susan began helping her mother in the kitchen when she was young and became proficient at cooking in her twenties. She is a self-taught watercolor artist but didn't paint her first picture until she was 30.

Lemon Pepper Tea Biscuits

Makes 1 dozen

- 1 (3-oz.) package cream cheese, softened
- ¼ cup butter, softened
- Grated zest of 1 lemon
- ½ cup sour cream
- 1 cup self-rising flour
- ⅓ cup dried cranberries, chopped
- Coarsely ground pepper
- Sanding sugar (optional)

1. Preheat oven to 400°F.

2. In a deep, medium-sized bowl, beat cream cheese, butter, and zest with mixer on medium speed until smooth. Scrape down bowl. Stir in sour cream. Gradually beat in flour until well blended. Scrape down bowl. Stir in cranberries.

3. Put a heaping tsp. of dough into each cup of an ungreased miniature muffin pan, filling the space completely and leveling the surface of the dough. Grind pepper over the top. Sprinkle with sanding sugar, if desired. Bake for 15 minutes, or until light brown. Pop out muffins into a basket lined with a tea towel. Cover to keep warm.

A few years later, she combined her love of cooking and her newfound hobby of watercolor art as she painted and wrote her first cookbook at the dining table of her little house on Martha's Vineyard. Susan was thrilled to find out her book was going to be published. A few months later, Susan received a letter with a return address she didn't recognize. She opened it while sitting in her car in the snowy post office parking lot. It was a fan letter, thanking her for writing the book. "I sat in the car and cried," said Susan. "I just wasn't expecting it. This connection to people was the frosting on the cake and a complete inspiration to do more."

Apricot Jam

Makes 4 half-pint jars

- 1 lb. dried apricots
- 1 (8-oz.) can crushed pineapple with juice
- 2 cups sugar
- 1 tsp. cinnamon

1. Put apricots in large saucepan, add water to barely cover, and cook over medium-high heat until soft. Remove apricots from water in saucepan, chop finely, and return to water in pan.

2. Stir in crushed pineapple with juice; bring to boil. Stir in sugar. Boil rapidly, stirring often, until thick. Toward end of cooking, stir in cinnamon. Bring to jellying point on candy thermometer, 220°F (drop 2° for every 1,000 feet above sea level). Pour into hot sterilized jars and seal.

Home Sweet Home is Homemade in more ways than one.

"Sometimes a kitchen table tea party ends with everyone hurrying back to work," Susan laughs, "and sometimes it goes on so long, it turns to Twine—tea, then wine, and other times … we go completely bad, Twine turns to Skip and Go Nakeds, the Dixie Chicks start singing Earl's Got to Die, and we find out where all the bodies are buried (not just Earl's!). Whatever would we do without our girlfriends!? I wouldn't want to know!"

*O*ld creamers make good flower vases.

Skip and Go Nakeds

Makes 2 servings

- ⅔ cup cold beer
- ⅔ cup frozen pink lemonade
- ¼ cup vodka

Fill a blender halfway with ice. Add beer, frozen lemonade, and vodka. Blend and serve.

Women are most fascinating between the ages of 35 and 40 after they have won a few races & know how to pace themselves. Since few women ever pass 40, maximum fascination can continue indefinitely. ♥ Christian Dior

A New Orleans SUNDAY JAZZ Brunch

Celebrating Soul in the Heart of Brooklyn

Orianne Cosentino

Orianne Cosentino is a chef and music lover with an eclectic circle of friends. Looking to take a break from life's usual pace, she hosted a New Orleans style jazz brunch at her home in Brooklyn, New York. An invitation was extended to a local musical trio who provided the perfect atmosphere for her Southern-style fare. In the glorious tapestry of New York City, Orianne's friends were able to catch up on one another's lives and easily found an abundance of things to celebrate on a crisp and luminous autumn Sunday.

I love serving food that is interactive. At the brunch, guests were building their own cocktails, cutting and sharing fruit on little cutting boards that were part of the centerpieces, and passing platters of roasted veggies. It makes everyone feel involved and hands-on ... a true community feast!

Hot Gruyère and Cider Dip

Makes about 3 cups

1	lb. Gruyère, shredded
½	cup Parmesan, grated
2	TB. all-purpose flour
2½	cups apple cider or juice
3	sprigs of rosemary
1	tsp. garlic powder
	Salt and pepper
2	TB. chopped chives, for garnish

1. Toss the Gruyère and the Parmesan with the flour to combine.

2. In a medium saucepan, bring the apple cider with rosemary sprigs to a rolling boil; reduce to a simmer.

3. Add the cheese and flour mixture and stir until the cheese is melted. Remove from heat and stir in the garlic powder. Add salt and pepper to taste. Transfer to a serving bowl or individual ramekins and top with chives. Serve immediately with an assortment of fruits, vegetables, or breads for dipping.

"I **took** the one **less traveled** by."
—Robert Frost

Seasonal ingredients are such a pleasure to use because they complement each other so well. There is the saying "if they grow together, they go together." And I believe it.

Orianne's jazz brunch menu nodded stylistically toward the South, but most of her ingredients were locally produced New York seasonals: striped squash, potatoes, kale, heaps of apples and pears picked at their peak, and collards so local she harvested them right out of her yard. Aromatic rosemary, sage, and thyme, plucked from clay pots, joined a variety of crazy gourds from the Community Supported Agriculture at her autumnal table. "We repurposed other little things that were sitting around, a few of the last ripening tomatoes, some plant clippings growing in water—the stuff that surrounds us in our everyday lives—and gave them a place of importance."

As friends piled in, jazz tunes heralded each entrance. Drinks were served from a short bar menu of Creole Bloody Marys, Abita beer, Sauvignon Blanc, cold-brewed coffee, and juice. In true New York fashion, almost everyone was involved in the art, music, and/or food and beverage industry. As the guests unwound and conversed, a number of personal celebrations came to light. The host and chef/hostess were expecting their first child, two guests were coincidentally celebrating their anniversary that weekend, and another couple was about to embark on an extended vacation after months of working hard at their summer business. Two other friends were celebrating their first free weekend in two years—they had just hired an employee for their vintage clothing shop. Glasses clinked to pleasant Sunday afternoons everywhere as the last guest burst through the door, directly from the airport, enormous suitcase in tow. Just in from a whirlwind three-week photo shoot in Georgia, she was back home in Brooklyn with a brunch party in full swing and a lovingly homemade meal about to be served.

For the first course, Orianne turned to Cajun chef Justin Wilson, most remembered for his fabulous accent and his PBS cooking show. His cookbook, a souvenir Orianne picked up on a trip to Louisiana, includes phonetic excerpts: "So don' forget, it ain't no sin to dunk. An' if it is, who give a dam' anyway?" On that recommendation, Orianne served a rosemary-scented Hot Gruyère and Cider Dip with a platter of roasted potato and squash wedges, toasted baguette, and fresh pears.

The main course was a riff on bacon and eggs; the bacon was replaced by a pork chop and the egg became a sort of French *sauce gribiche* (a mayonnaise-style cold egg sauce) consisting of a fine dice of hard-cooked eggs, mayo, caper, and pickle that was spooned on top of the chop. Supporting the pork-and-egg combo were braised greens with apple, a sweet/tart combination cooked with a touch of sugar and a splash of vinegar in the Southern tradition.

More authentic New Orleans fare followed: Bananas Foster (invented in 1951 at Brennan's Restaurant) and homemade Coffee Ice Cream flavored with Café Du Monde's coffee-chicory blend. Walnuts toasted with ginger, maple, and Tony Chachere's Original Creole Seasoning made another play on "the sweet and the heat" so often found in Big Easy delicacies.

From enjoying the fall harvest to conquering the daily grind, Orianne and her friends take the relaxed approach. "We can conjure up a celebration," she says, "at the drop of a leaf."

Bananas Foster

Pork Chops & Eggs

Braised Greens and Apples

Serves 4

- 1 lb. mixed dark leafy greens (kale, collards, chard, etc.)
- 2 TB. oil
- ½ cup chopped onion
- 2 cloves garlic, minced
- 1 apple, cored and chopped
- ¼ cup apple cider vinegar
- ¼ cup water
- 1 TB. sugar
- Salt and pepper

1. Remove stems from greens, wash thoroughly, and chop into bite-sized pieces.

2. Heat the oil in a large skillet. Add the onion, garlic, and apple and sauté for 1 minute.

3. Add the greens and stir until wilted. Add the vinegar, water, and sugar, mixing until well combined. Simmer until the liquid is almost evaporated and the greens and apples are tender, about 10 minutes. Season with salt and pepper to taste.

"Change It AROUND" Party

A New Year's Eve Devoted to People

Sandy Coughlin

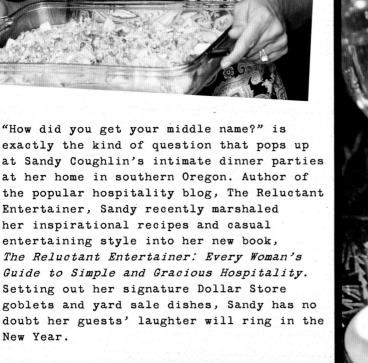

"How did you get your middle name?" is exactly the kind of question that pops up at Sandy Coughlin's intimate dinner parties at her home in southern Oregon. Author of the popular hospitality blog, The Reluctant Entertainer, Sandy recently marshaled her inspirational recipes and casual entertaining style into her new book, *The Reluctant Entertainer: Every Woman's Guide to Simple and Gracious Hospitality*. Setting out her signature Dollar Store goblets and yard sale dishes, Sandy has no doubt her guests' laughter will ring in the New Year.

When traditions start making you feel like you have no choice, Sandy Coughlin knows it's time to spice things up a bit. "Feeling forced to entertain over the holidays is no fun for anyone," says Sandy. "To get out of it, people end up making excuses, saying it's too expensive or too much work."

But Sandy's philosophy is that the party isn't about you or your house—it is about you and your guests getting together for some fun. "I ask myself who I would want to spend five hours with and which of my friends would enjoy connecting to one another." Sandy jots down her notes and ideas in a little pocket notebook that keeps everything at her fingertips: menu, seating arrangements, who is bringing the salad, her grocery list. "By using what you have, borrowing what you don't have, and delegating some of the work, you can make giving a party doable and fun."

One of Sandy's New Year's Eve Parties will be a sit-down, four-course dinner for eighteen guests. Sandy puts two tables end to end and covers them with two matching tablecloths from a discount store. Black and white chairs were borrowed from a friend. The table is set with Dollar Store goblets and yard sale dishes on alternating gold and silver chargers. Fresh red Gerber daisies and inexpensive tea lights prove that entertaining can be attainable, easy, and elegant in any setting.

"The key to a successful party is smart planning," says Sandy. Her invitation lets guests know they are attending a "casual-dressy" sit-down dinner because "people are less likely to cancel and more likely to show up on time" than for a buffet. A clear invitation avoids embarrassment all around. Sandy always chooses a main course that can be made a day or two ahead and sticks with familiar dishes so that food preparation doesn't consume the party day. Place cards are tied around the water goblets, and she writes the name of each guest with a permanent fine-point marker on the base of each wine glass.

Tip: Garnish with your favorite herb. In our case, we used lovage from our garden.

Carrot Orange Soup

Serves 6
(recipe can be doubled or tripled)
Adapted from *The Reluctant Entertainer*

- 4 TB. butter
- 2 cups finely chopped yellow onions (I use sweet onions)
- 12 large carrots (1½ to 2 lb.), peeled and chopped
- 4 cups chicken stock, divided
- 1 cup fresh orange juice
- Salt and freshly ground pepper
- Freshly grated orange zest

1. In a large saucepan or kettle, melt butter over low heat. Add onions and sauté for 25 minutes.

2. Add carrots and 2 cups of the chicken stock to onions. Bring to a boil, reduce heat, and simmer for 30 minutes.

3. Blend the mixture in a blender or food processor to the texture you prefer. Return purée to the saucepan and add remaining 2 cups stock and orange juice. Season with salt, pepper, and zest. Serve hot.

Pecan Pear Cranberry Green Salad

Serves 6

Salad

- ½ cup chopped pecans
- 1 (10- to 14-oz.) package fresh spinach or garden greens (washed and ready to eat)
- 1 or 2 ripe Bartlett pears, cored, quartered, and sliced
- ½ cup dried cranberries
- ¼ red onion, thinly sliced
- 1 avocado, peeled and diced
- ½ cup feta, crumbled

Dressing

- ⅔ cup oil
- ⅔ cup sugar
- ¼ cup cider vinegar
- 2 TB. balsamic vinegar
- ¼ cup lemon juice
- 3 TB. poppy seeds
- 1 tsp. salt
- ¼ cup chopped onion

1. Toast pecans and set aside to cool.

2. Combine salad ingredients (except pecans) in a large bowl.

3. Combine dressing ingredients in a small bowl and mix well. Drizzle the dressing (to taste) over the salad; add in the cooled pecans. Toss together and serve.

With fun music playing, guests begin to arrive and mingle as Sandy and a few friends put the finishing touches on dinner. During a first course of carrot orange soup, the evening really gets rolling. Guests must each answer the question, "What's your middle name and how did you get it?" People have fun learning about each other, and the conversation never lags.

The second course is where the "change it around" part of the party begins. With the music volume amped up, everyone leaves the room and a few of Sandy's friends transform the table with fresh napkins, fresh plates of salad, and a change in the placement of everyone's wine and water glasses. The idea is to seat each guest next to someone new. When guests return, they find a penny under each water goblet. Each guest announces the year the penny was minted, comes up with a significant event that happened to them that same year, and the conversation takes off a second time.

No-peel Apple Cake

Makes 8 to 10 servings

Adapted from *The Reluctant Entertainer*

- 4 cups chopped, unpeeled apples (half-inch pieces)
- ½ cup oil
- ½ cup applesauce (or apple butter)
- 1¾ cups sugar, divided
- 2 eggs
- 2 cups flour
- 1 tsp. salt
- 2 tsp. cinnamon
- 2 tsp. baking soda
- ½ cup chopped pecans

1. Preheat oven to 350°F. Grease a 9 x 13-inch baking dish.

2. In a large bowl, combine apples, oil, applesauce, 1½ cups of the sugar, eggs, flour, salt, cinnamon, and baking soda and mix well.

3. Pour batter into baking dish. Sprinkle pecans and remaining ¼ cup sugar over the top. Bake for 50 minutes, or until skewer inserted in the center comes out clean. Let the cake cool for about 15 minutes before serving. Cut into pieces and serve on plates with a dab of freshly whipped cream on top. If desired, drizzle with caramel sauce.

"Ponder **well** on this point: the **pleasant** hours of our life are all **connected** by a more or less tangible link, with some memory of the **table**."
— Charles Pierre Monselet
(1825-1888)

30

Chocolate-dipped Bacon

Serves 6 to 8

- 6 to 8 slices thick-cut, best-quality bacon
- 12 oz. semisweet chocolate chips or your favorite chocolate

1. Preheat the oven to 375°F. Place bacon on a baking sheet lined with parchment paper. Bake in oven to desired doneness; bacon should not be too soft nor so crisp that it breaks easily. Cool on the parchment paper for 5 minutes and then transfer to a plate lined with paper towels.

2. Line another baking sheet with parchment paper. Melt chocolate in a double boiler or on low in the microwave. Using tongs, carefully dip a bacon strip halfway into the melted chocolate, turning it to coat all sides, and set on parchment. Repeat with each remaining slice of bacon.

3. Refrigerate 1 hour or until chocolate is hard. Arrange on a tiered serving dish. Serve the same day as a savory and sweet appetizer, before dessert or as a mini dessert.

After the second course, music once again fills the air, guests get up, and the table is transformed for the main course. Everyone returns to a new seat, an entrée of beef Wellington, and a juicy new topic: your first French kiss. The unexpectedness of the questions and responses is what makes the party fun. "While I am preparing the dessert," says Sandy, "one of the guys put on some 1970s tunes and everyone started dancing to all the songs we love." Dessert is a delicious apple cake with cream and caramel on top. And what is a New Year's celebration without bacon dipped in melted chocolate? While munching on the sweets, the guests have the chance to answer the last topic of the evening: Tell us about your first and favorite concert.

Laughter, sharing stories, acceptance, and the connection to existing and new friendships form the basis of hospitality. Feelings of inadequacy, unrealistic expectations, fear of failure, and lack of time all conspire to steal the joy that comes from opening one's home to others. "Fear is often a jail cell," says Sandy, "locking us in so that we don't form friendships. Friends bring zest to life. Without friendship, we become lonely, isolated, and smaller than we want and need to be."

BACK in the DAY Bakery

Cheryl Day

Cheryl Day started as a home baker, and she's determined to keep the art of scratch baking alive and well in America. This enterprising, passionate artisan opened Back in the Day Bakery in Savannah, Georgia, in 2002 with her husband Griff. Today, they are working on a cookbook that celebrates the good wholesome ingredients and time-tested family recipes that have made their urban neighborhood bakery a unique destination.

33

"... if you **love** what you do, then the **world** will fall in love with **you**."

—Chuck Williams, Williams-Sonoma

Old-Fashioned Cupcakes with Vanilla Buttercream Frosting

Makes 24 cupcakes

1¾ cups cake flour (not self-rising)

1¼ cups unbleached all-purpose flour

2 cups sugar

1 TB. baking powder

¾ tsp. salt

1 cup (2 sticks) unsalted butter, at room temperature, cut into cubes

4 large eggs, at room temperature

1 cup whole milk

1 tsp. pure vanilla extract

Vanilla Buttercream Frosting (recipe on next page)

Old-Fashioned Hand-Tinted Sprinkles (recipe on next page)

1. Preheat oven to 325°F. Line cupcake pans with paper liners.

2. Add flours, sugar, baking powder, and salt to a large mixing bowl. Mix on low speed for 3 minutes until well combined.

3. Add butter and continue mixing on low speed until the mixture resembles course sand.

4. Add eggs one at a time, mixing on medium speed after each addition until combined.

5. Slowly add milk and vanilla to batter and continue mixing, scraping down the bowl, until thoroughly combined.

6. Scoop batter into baking cups, filling each about two-thirds full. Bake for 17 to 20 minutes or until a cake tester inserted in the center comes out clean.

7. Cool and decorate with frosting and sprinkles.

It was no surprise to family and friends that Cheryl Day grew up to own a bakery. Cheryl has always enjoyed feeding crowds of people who express their appreciation with smiling faces, laughter, and happy tummies. In Savannah, Georgia, the Hostess City of the South, residents and visitors alike keep coming back to taste Back in the Day Bakery's delicious, nostalgic treats.

Part of what makes Cheryl's avocation so much fun is being part of people's memory-making occasions. Cheryl loves celebrations. When she was young, she pulled out the party section of every *Seventeen* magazine. She saved pages of tips, recipes, and festive decorating ideas in a notebook and gathered ideas in her head for all the future parties she would throw for family and friends when she grew up. By paying attention to these pages and the gracious example set by her parents, who were known for their lively parties, Cheryl learned that any event, from a simple lunch for two to a wedding reception, could leave guests with special memories that would keep them talking for years.

Artist Jenn Hayslip approached Cheryl about hosting a Southern-themed cupcake party at the bakery for her Petticoats and Parasols Vendor Fair in April 2010. The two women worked closely together to make the cheerful, vintage industrial vibe of the neighborhood bakery the backdrop for this gathering of creative women. The fair was the first event of that scale to be held in the bakery, so Cheryl used her three time-tested pointers for party planning.

PERFECT PARTY PLANNING:

1. Meet your match.

Cheryl sits down for lengthy conversations with customers about the details they already envision or have planned for their event. She asks that they bring photos so that they can begin to visualize special details that will make the party unique, personal, and memorable. Cheryl is known for her signature vintage style and comforting, home-baked aesthetic, and her customers usually want to adapt some version of that look and feel for their special occasion. Cheryl suggests you assemble a team of people who share your vision.

2. Set the tone.

When planning a celebration, every detail matters, from start to finish. Jenn had wonderful cards and posters printed well in advance of the fair that evoked the tradition of Southern belles and the Ford Plantation. This grand antebellum home outside of Savannah, purchased in the 1930s by automobile magnate Henry Ford for his winter residence, was the site of Jenn's weekend-long workshop for creative women. Her invitation set the tone of the party and let guests know what to expect when they arrived.

3. Set the scene.

Back in the Day Bakery offers its own magical ambiance with vintage crystal chandeliers and brightly colored garlands, flags, and paper lanterns draping the windows. The circa 1925 building, formerly the Starland Dairy General Store, sits in an urban neighborhood that provided a perfect complement to the sweeping vistas of the Ford Plantation. The many vintage-inspired products offered for sale at the event and the wonderful whimsical confections that the vendors wore combined to create an enchanted evening.

That kind of enchantment is what stays with people and causes them to return to the bakery time and again. Cheryl loves it when couples come back years after the wedding, children in tow, to order an anniversary cake the entire family can enjoy. It lets her know that she helped create a family tradition. No matter how big or small the event, she always takes the same amount of time and care in the planning process. For Cheryl, it is all about creating lasting memories.

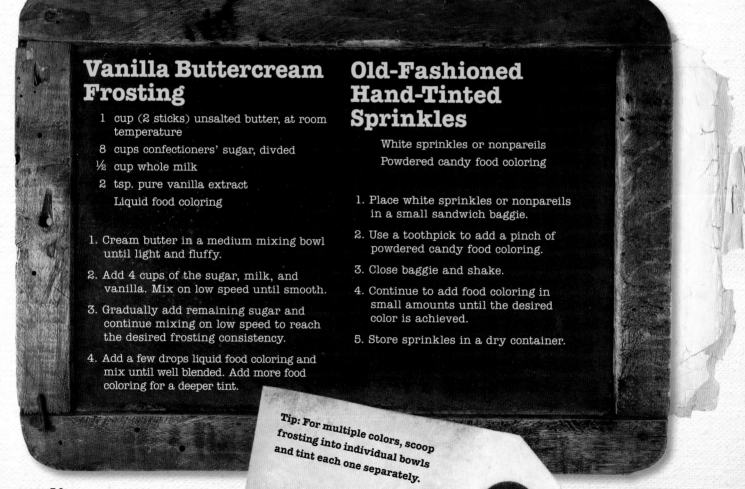

Vanilla Buttercream Frosting

1 cup (2 sticks) unsalted butter, at room temperature

8 cups confectioners' sugar, divded

½ cup whole milk

2 tsp. pure vanilla extract

Liquid food coloring

1. Cream butter in a medium mixing bowl until light and fluffy.

2. Add 4 cups of the sugar, milk, and vanilla. Mix on low speed until smooth.

3. Gradually add remaining sugar and continue mixing on low speed to reach the desired frosting consistency.

4. Add a few drops liquid food coloring and mix until well blended. Add more food coloring for a deeper tint.

Old-Fashioned Hand-Tinted Sprinkles

White sprinkles or nonpareils

Powdered candy food coloring

1. Place white sprinkles or nonpareils in a small sandwich baggie.

2. Use a toothpick to add a pinch of powdered candy food coloring.

3. Close baggie and shake.

4. Continue to add food coloring in small amounts until the desired color is achieved.

5. Store sprinkles in a dry container.

Tip: For multiple colors, scoop frosting into individual bowls and tint each one separately.

Slow down and taste the sweet life.

CUPCAKES

37

Dinner
with MY DADDY
A Wednesday Ritual

Marina Drasnin

Marina Drasnin is a painter,
a decorator, a florist, an
entertainer, a mother, a loving
wife, and a devoted daughter to her
sweet and precious father. Every
Wednesday is a celebration of their
memories, their time together, and
their love for one another.

Marina Drasnin is the first to admit it—she's a daddy's girl! Sidney Mitchell Drasnin was, and will always be, her first love. "I am the middle daughter of five children, 'Three,' as he likes to call me with a grin!"

Marina's precious daddy is a man whose great sense of humor and joie de vivre walk into the room before he does. He has devoted his entire adult life to his family. He knows what true love looks like, having been married happily to Marina's mother, Virginia, for 55 years. "There is so much to admire and love about this man," says Marina, reflecting on his life as a renowned architect, proficient pilot, expert sailor, world traveler, and so much more, "but it is his curiosity, his wonderment for knowledge and life, that continues to amaze everybody around him—even at his tender young age of 90!"

Marina lost her mother almost three years ago, and not a day goes by that she doesn't miss and think about her. "She was sublime. A beauty inside and out." And of course this sentiment goes without saying for her daddy. He adored Virginia—they were the best of friends.

So it has been in the past three years, come rain or shine, that Marina's daddy comes to her kitchen every Wednesday. Marina always prepares a beautiful meal and sets a colorful and happy table. Their time together is priceless, partly because his vantage point and wisdom on life is a gift beyond measure. "I always look forward to seeing him, and the time seems to fly by. Sometimes it is the two of us and his wonderful caretakers, Rosa and Carmela, but more often than not, I invite close friends to join me in this weekly celebration of my daddy's unique spirit."

"The **world** is your **oyster**."
—Favorite quote of my dad's

Marina believes that people have lost the art of storytelling in this age of technology and quick fixes. As her father shares his stories, it reminds her to slow down, to be present, and not to worry about the small things in life. "I promise you that no one leaves our Wednesday afternoon lunches without a kiss and hug for both daddy and me and a sincere thank-you for being included. To be the daughter and friend of this gracious and divine human being is certainly equivalent to, if not better than, a lottery win!"

Celebrating and sharing her father—it is Marina's gift and also her greatest joy.

Sidney's Stuffed Acorns

Makes 12 servings

- 6 acorn squash
- 12 TB. butter
- 12 TB. firmly packed brown sugar
- 6 tsp. cinnamon
  Salt and pepper
  Uncle Harry's Israeli Couscous (see recipe at right)

1. Preheat oven to 350°F. Cut each acorn squash in half lengthwise. Clean out the insides and discard all the seeds. Place halves on one or two large baking sheets, cut side down. Bake in preheated oven for 30 minutes.

2. Turn squash cut side up. Dot each acorn half with 1 TB. butter and sprinkle on 1 TB. brown sugar and ½ tsp. cinnamon in their center and bake for 20 minutes more. Season with salt and pepper to taste. Spoon some couscous into each half. Serve any remaining couscous on the side.

Harry's Israeli Couscous

Makes 12 servings (for acorn squash)

- 1 (6- to 8-oz.) package or box of Israeli couscous (sold at specialty markets)
- 1 tsp. chicken bouillon paste
- ½ cup dried cranberries
- ½ cup pecans or walnuts, preferably candied
- 1 apple or pear, cut into small cubes

1. Cook the Israeli couscous, following the directions on the package and add the chicken bouillon paste to the boiling water used for cooking.

2. When couscous is done, toss in dried cranberries, pecans or walnuts, and pear or apple cubes.

4th of July
in the Country
Ree Drummond

The Fourth of July is the time for an annual celebration at the home of Ree Drummond, the Pioneer Woman--a time when they put aside all the work of the ranch, get all the mowing and weeding accomplished, and welcome friends and relatives for a big summer meal and a night of colorful, explosive fireworks.

"Everyone's welcome at our Fourth of July celebration," says Ree. "A couple of weeks before the party, we stand up during the announcements at church and invite the whole congregation. We see acquaintances at the store in the week leading up to the Fourth and say 'Come on over!' Our cowboys are welcome, as well as their friends and families. And every in-law and cousin within a fifty-mile radius is required to attend."

In fact, what Ree loves most about the guests that assemble at their party is that they never really know who's going to show up! "I could never begin to orchestrate who will mingle well with whom, and I always get a kick out of seeing the 85-year-old ladies from church sitting at a picnic table with the teenage son of one of our cowboys, having a good conversation over burgers. I just sit back and watch, and smile."

Ree admits she could spend a lot of time, energy, and money decking out her house and surrounding area with flower arrangements, tablecloths, and napkins … "but why?" she asks. She'd rather sink her focus into the food and the fun. Those handheld American flags from the dollar store cover a multitude of decorating sins! Ree usually fills a few coffee cans with sunflowers, hands the kids the flags, and says, "Go for it!"

For the first few years of the party, Ree tried to map out and control the entire menu. "If guests called to ask what they could bring," she says, "I made a list and carefully assigned people certain categories of food so we'd have a nice, even distribution. Then one year, I just decided to throw caution to the wind and said 'bring whatever you'd like!' I was amazed that despite the complete lack of coordination and planning, everything turned out just fine."

Jalapeño Poppers

Makes 20 appetizers

I make as many of these as I have the time to make! We serve them as appetizers and put 'em on top of burgers!

20 whole, fresh jalapeños, 2 to 3 inches long
2 (8-oz.) packages cream cheese, softened
1 lb. thin (regular) bacon, sliced crosswise into thirds

1. Preheat oven to 375°F. Set out a baking pan with a rack.

2. Slip on some latex gloves, if you have them. Cut each jalapeño in half lengthwise. Use a spoon to remove the seeds and white membrane (the source of the heat). Leave a little membrane if you like things hot.

3. Smear softened cream cheese into each jalapeño half. Wrap each jalapeño with a piece of bacon (one third of a slice). Secure by sticking a toothpick through the middle. Set jalapeños on the baking pan rack. Bake for 30 to 45 minutes, or until bacon is chewy. Serve immediately or at room temperature.

45

Ree's husband grills burgers or steaks on a large grill, and they always make more than they know they'll need to ensure leftovers in the coming days! Ree and her sister-in-law make jalapeño poppers in enormous quantities. Guests devour them as they arrive, then pile them on top of their burgers when dinner's ready. They disappear as quickly as Ree can make them.

Ree also makes up a few basic sides in large quantities: baked beans, potato salad, and a bunch of fresh corn casserole. Missy makes delicious marinated tomatoes that Ree says "I could eat every day of my life." Once the sides are made, the only thing left is for the guests to arrive. They show up with macaroni and cheese, barbecue ribs, cole slaw, green salads, stuffed mushrooms … the list goes on and on.

"**Love** is a fruit in **season** at all times, and within **reach** of every **hand**."

—Mother Teresa

As for dessert, Ree always makes homemade ice cream the day before the party—everything from peach to vanilla to blackberry, "depending on what fruits I have available. Then, again, I let the guests take over: they show up with Italian cream cakes and fruit cobblers and pie and cookies and cakes. Fourth of July is no time to diet."

Ree loves adding cold blackberries to her lemonade: "sets it apart a bit," she says. "And finally, for the adventurous among us, I make a vat of an alcoholic 'punch' of some kind—either sangria or a fruit punch with vodka or rum. I'm careful to caution guests about how 'flammable' the drink is. Because of the sweet, fruity flavor, the taste of the alcohol can be masked—designated drivers are often needed!"

Firecracker Shrimp

Makes 6 servings

1 lb. raw jumbo shrimp
2 TB. Sriracha hot chili sauce
2 TB. olive oil
¼ tsp. salt
2 tsp. sugar
5 cloves garlic, pressed

1. Peel and devein the shrimp.

2. Combine chili sauce, olive oil, salt, sugar, and garlic in a large resealable plastic bag. Add the shrimp and marinate for 20 minutes to 2 hours.

3. Skewer shrimp and cook over a hot grill until opaque and brown, with black bits. Serve and watch them disappear!

Through the years, Ree's learned a lot about entertaining a large summer crowd, and she's run the gamut from stressed and hectic to calm, cool, and collected. The turning point was the year she was pregnant with their third child: "I was big and uncomfortable and couldn't have overachieved if I'd tried. And that year wound up being the most fun ever."

"I cannot emphasize this enough: Fourth of July, more than any other holiday, can and should be casual, easy, and fun. I've learned that guests won't ever leave your party with a checklist of how many perfectly folded gingham napkins you had or what kind of flowers adorned your tables. What they'll leave with, hopefully, is a warm glow—not from the 95-degree summer heat (though that's surely a factor), but from the time spent with friends."

Food, family, friends, and smiles: strip everything else away, and those are the things that really matter.

Cake POP Party

Celebrating the Creative Spirit on a Stick!

Angie Dudley
BAKERELLA

"Everything tastes better on a stick!" says Angie Dudley, author of the *New York Times* Best Seller's List, *Cake Pops*, a beautifully photographed book of … well … "cake balls on a stick." Raised in Atlanta, Georgia, Angie's popular book signing tour took her coast to coast where she met and celebrated with other cake ball enthusiasts. In her sought-after cake pop classes, Angie not only teaches how to create the perfect pop, but how creating memories together is a celebration in of itself.

With just about every celebration, a delicious cake is included at some point in the festivities. With Angie Dudley, her cake pops, are the reason for the celebration or gathering in the first place. "They just make people so happy," Angie says with a big smile. Author of *Cake Pops*, Angie's edible pop art is just the creative outlet that brings the young and the young at heart, mothers and daughters, new friends and old friends together to celebrate relationships or special events.

Cupcake Camps are popping up everywhere and Cake Pop classes are fast becoming a popular way for people to create in a fun, new setting. At this particular Cupcake Camp, held at NYE Beach Market, in Newport, Oregon, Angie teaches several dozen, eager participants who are there to grow in creative spirit as well as in friendships. "It is wonderful to see young children so interested in baking," says Angie. The room is filled with laughter as each try to dip, roll, and poke their cake balls.

Basic Cupcake Pops

Makes 4 dozen

Not only can you make cake balls and turn them into cake pops, but you can also mold them into other shapes using a small metal cookie cutter. Keep color scheme in mind when shopping for frosting and cake mixes. For these cupcake pops, use a flower-shaped cookie cutter. Take them to the next level of cuteness by using more than one color of candy coating and adding sprinkles and candy for decoration.

1 (18.25-oz.) box cake mix
1 (16-oz.) container ready-made frosting
32 ozs. white candy coating
48 paper lollipop sticks
16 ozs. yellow candy coating
   M&M's or similarly shaped candy
   Sprinkles
   Styrofoam block to dry and stand pops

1. Bake the cake as directed on the cake mix package, using a 9 x 13-inch cake pan. Let cool completely.

2. Cut the cake into four equal sections. Remove a section from the pan, break it in half, and rub the two pieces together over a large bowl, making sure to crumble any large pieces that fall off. You can also use a fork to break any larger pieces of cake apart. Repeat with each section until the entire cake is crumbled into a fine texture. You should not see any large pieces of cake. If you have large pieces mixed in, the cake balls may turn out lumpy and bumpy.

3. Add three-quarters of the container of frosting. (If you used the entire container, the cake balls would be too moist.) Mix the frosting into the crumbled cake, using the back of a large spoon, until thoroughly combined. The mixture should be moist enough to roll into 1½-inch balls and hold a round shape.

4. Line a baking sheet with waxed paper. Roll 48 cake balls by hand and place them on the baking sheet. Cover with plastic wrap and chill for several hours in the refrigerator or place in the freezer for about 15 minutes. The balls should be firm but not frozen.

5. Remove the baking sheet from the refrigerator or freezer and begin shaping the chilled cake balls into cupcakes. Roll a cake ball into a cylinder shape and then slide it into a flower-shaped cookie cutter. The cake mixture should fill the entire cutter. Use your thumb to keep the shape flat on one side and allow any excess to form a mounded cupcake top on the other side. When the cupcake is shaped in a way you like, gently push it out of the cutter from the bottom (or gently pull it out from the top mounded side) and place it back on the baking sheet lined with waxed paper. Continue until all of the cake balls are shaped. Return the baking sheet to the freezer for 5 to 10 minutes to keep the cupcakes firm.

6. Place half of the white candy coating in a deep, microwave-safe plastic bowl. These bowls make it easier to dip the cupcake bottoms completely in candy coating while holding the bowl without burning your fingers. Following the package directions, microwave on medium power for 30 seconds at a time, stirring with a spoon in between, to melt the white candy. You can also use a double boiler. Either way, make sure you do not overheat the coating.

7. Now you're ready to dip. Take a few shaped cupcakes out of the freezer to work with and transfer the rest to the refrigerator so they stay firm but do not freeze. Line a second baking sheet with waxed paper. Hold a cupcake by the mounded top and dip the bottom into the melted white candy coating—just to the point where the mounded shape starts. Remove it from the white candy, turn it upside down, and swirl your hand in a circular motion. This swirling motion will cause any excess white coating to slide down onto the bottom of the mounded top. Once it does that, you can stop swirling. Keep a dish towel handy to wipe the white candy off your fingertips; don't use water to rinse your hands, as getting water in the coating can make it unusable.

8. Place the half-coated cupcake shape on the second baking sheet, white candy side up and mounded side down. Immediately dip the tip of a lollipop stick into the melted candy, coating about ½ inch of the stick, and then insert the coated end of the stick straight into the flat, white-coated bottom of the cupcake while the white candy is still wet. Push it no more than halfway through. Continue with the rest of the cupcake-shaped cake balls. Allow the white candy to dry completely.

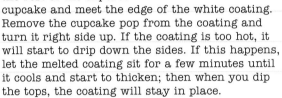

9. Melt the yellow candy coating in the same way that you melted the white candy. You will now decorate the tops. This all comes together quickly, resulting in a finished cupcake pop. Holding a cupcake by its lollipop stick, dip the top of a cupcake in the melted yellow candy coating. It should completely cover the rest of the exposed cupcake and meet the edge of the white coating. Remove the cupcake pop from the coating and turn it right side up. If the coating is too hot, it will start to drip down the sides. If this happens, let the melted coating sit for a few minutes until it cools and start to thicken; then when you dip the tops, the coating will stay in place.

10. While the yellow coating is still wet, use a toothpick to touch up any areas the coating may not have covered. Then place an M&M (M-side down) on the top and add sprinkles for decoration.

11. Set the stick end of the cupcake pop in a block of Styrofoam to dry completely. Repeat with the remaining cupcake pops. Store the cupcake pops in an airtight container on the counter or in the refrigerator for several days. You can also cover them in small treat bags, tied with a ribbon, and leave them in the Styrofoam block on the counter.

Tips

- Make the cake the day before and let it cool overnight. Then you can do the crumbling, rolling, shaping, dipping, and decorating on the second day.

- You can also leave uncoated cake balls, covered in plastic wrap, in the refrigerator overnight if you want to do the dipping on the following day.

- You can make these without lollipop sticks. They're just as cute.

- Don't get any water in the candy coating. Keep your hands completely dry. Water will mess up the coating and ruin all your hard work.

- Poke holes in the Styrofoam drying block stand *before* you start dipping, using a lollipop stick. Leave enough space between the holes so the cakes won't touch.

- Experiment with different candy coating color combinations.

- Try this technique with other small cookie cutters, such as hearts or butterflies.

- Place sprinkles in a small dish and pinch a few with your fingers to sprinkle on top of the pops. Sprinkle over a large bowl to reuse any that fall.

Angie is generous with giving out her tips. "The finer the crumbs, the smoother the ball," she shares with the class. She continues, "Dip the ball, don't swirl it. Swirling isn't good. Dip straight down and tap off the excess coating." She explains she didn't come from a family of bakers nor has formal training, she "just liked to bake." Her journey began with a cake decorating class. "I always liked to bake growing up. But I didn't really decorate before I started blogging," Angie says. On her blog, Bakerella, she photographs her cupcakes, cake pops, and other treats while offering recipes and baking tips. It is an inspirational and fun blog where Angie not only shares her edible creations, but she is also honest about her baking mishaps as well. The joy she gets out of creating and sharing is evident in her cheerful blog. Her ability to relate to her readers is what keeps them coming back for more "eye-popping" photos and baking tips.

It is this form of creating and sharing that others have noted and are taking into their own homes in a form of a party. "It is empowering," says Angie. "So often, you walk by a bakery window and think you can't do that, but with these cake pops, you really can make them!" she says excitedly. "It is so easy, it can be done anywhere," Angie explains. "You don't even have to bake a cake, you can buy one already made and just make pops with it in your own kitchen," she says. A simple plastic bowl for the candy coating, frosting, a bowl to crumble the cake, and lollipop sticks, and basically, a Cake Pop Party is in the making. No fancy equipment needed or large space. Just fun friends with a creative spirit, who want an excuse to eat cake, and a party is on its way!

Back at the Cupcake Camp, a young girl shows a little owl she made to Angie with pride. Angie responds with pure excitement. The small girl is filled with joy at her sense of accomplishment as she carefully carries her owl after proudly showing it to Angie. It is this kind of interaction between children and adults that Cake Pop Parties tend to bring out in everyone. Sharing, creating, showing, and encouraging. Angie continues with her tips as the class is all abuzz with excitement about cake, candy coating, and crumbling.

And that is what celebrating should be all about: excitement. "People tend to open up more when they are learning something fun," explains Angie. "It is a great creative outlet for anyone, young and old," she says. Angie's talent goes far beyond creating beautiful edible pop art. She has a talent for gathering people of all ages and backgrounds together for one happy purpose: to celebrate the creative spirit...on a stick!

"life is sweet."

—Angie Dudley

"NUGGET" Warming

A Green Baby Shower

Ashley English

Ashley English wears a lot of hats. She sports a country homestead hat living with her husband, chickens, bees, dogs, and cats in the tiny mountain town of Candler, North Carolina. She's the author of The *Homemade Living* series of books *Canning and Preserving*, *Keeping Chickens*, *Home Dairy*, and *Keeping Bees* and pens a weekly blog posting for Design*Sponge. When she donned the new hat of motherhood, she naturally decided to celebrate the Ashley English way.

Ashley English enjoys a sustainable lifestyle that is the envy of many. "If you have a kitchen, a backyard, a stoop, or a roof, you can do it," says Ashley. Living on a small mountain homestead, Ashley bakes, cans, cooks, writes, gardens, blogs, raises chickens, and is a beekeeper, all while being married and raising her new baby.

Like many people, Ashley didn't know exactly what she wanted to do with her life. Living in Washington, D.C., she discovered "politics and social awareness," earned degrees in sociology and nutrition, and worked for nonprofit organizations dedicated to social and agricultural issues. Back home in North Carolina, she found work as a medical assistant and nutrition consultant. When she met and married Glenn, she moved onto his 12-acre "farm" located on Sunray Cove in the Blue Ridge Mountains. The previous owner had used the land as an edible herb and flower farm. It had several outbuildings, none of them in good shape, and the land hadn't been farmed since who knows when.

(Continued on page 60.)

Butternut Squash and Gorgonzola Pasta with Seasonal Pumpkin Seed Pesto

Serves 6 to 8

1 large butternut squash, peeled and cubed

Salt and freshly ground pepper

½ cup olive oil, plus more for roasting and cooking

1 cup raw pumpkin seeds

4 cloves garlic, finely minced

½ lemon and zest from peel

1 cup fresh whole sage leaves (or a mixture of ½ cup sage leaves and ½ cup lemon balm leaves)

1 lb. fusilli

¾ cup crumbled Gorgonzola

2 TB. capers

1. Toss cubed butternut squash with a pinch each of salt and pepper and a couple of TB. of olive oil. Roast in a shallow 11 x 7-inch baking pan in a 400°F oven for 30 minutes until tender. Remove from oven and set aside.

2. While squash is roasting, toast pumpkin seeds in a couple of TB. olive oil over medium heat until some of the seeds start to lightly brown. Add garlic, lemon zest, and a pinch of salt and pepper to the pumpkin seeds and cook for 2 more minutes. Remove from heat and allow mixture to cool for a few minutes.

3. Chop sage (or sage and lemon balm) finely in food processor. Add two-thirds of the pumpkin seed mixture, lemon juice, and ½ cup olive oil to the sage and puree until smooth.

4. Cook the pasta according to package instructions. Drain pasta and stir Gorgonzola into pasta until fully melted. Stir in the sage pesto, capers, squash, and remaining pumpkin seed mixture. Serve warm or at room temperature.

Sugared Molasses Crinkles

Makes 2 dozen

- 2½ cups all-purpose flour
- 1½ tsp. baking soda
- 1 tsp. sea salt
- 1½ tsp. ground cinnamon
- 1½ tsp. ground ginger
- 1 tsp. ground nutmeg
- ½ tsp. ground cloves
- ½ tsp. ground black pepper
- 1 cup dark brown sugar
- ¾ cup granulated sugar, divided
- ½ cup (1 stick) butter, at room temperature
- 2 eggs
- ⅓ cup molasses

1. Sift together flour, baking soda, salt, cinnamon, ginger, nutmeg, cloves, and black pepper in a medium-sized mixing bowl. Set aside.

2. Using an electric mixer, beat brown sugar, ¼ cup of the granulated sugar, and butter until thoroughly combined. Beat in eggs one at a time, stopping after each addition to scrape down sides of bowl. Beat in molasses until completely incorporated.

3. Reduce speed to low and gradually add flour mixture, stopping to scrape down sides of bowl. Continue mixing just until all flour is incorporated and a dough forms; do not overmix. Remove bowl from mixer and cover with plastic wrap, a kitchen cloth, or a dinner plate. Refrigerate for 1 hour.

4. Preheat oven to 350°F. Line cookie sheets with parchment paper. Place remaining ½ cup granulated sugar in a shallow bowl. Form chilled dough into 1-inch balls (about 1 TB. of dough), roll in sugar, and place on cookie sheets about 3 inches apart. Bake until centers are firm, 12 to 15 minutes. Cool 5 minutes on cookie sheets, transfer to wire cooling racks, and allow to cool completely. Store in an airtight container. Best when served within 4 to 5 days.

With a blank canvas before her and a passion for seasonal, organically grown food, Ashley quit her job and took a leap of faith. An opportunity to write about small-scale homesteading came about through a friend at Lark Crafts. Ashley could use her acreage and her background in nutrition to teach about seasonal and local foods. The publisher suggested canning and keeping chickens as first topics, and Ashley thought, why not? She had helped with canning as a child at her maternal grandmother's blueberry farm, and she also kept a flock of chickens. For the next year and a half, she immersed herself in research and writing.

To welcome their new baby, Ashley and Glenn invited family and friends to a green baby shower—a "Nugget Warming." During Ashley's pregnancy, the couple started calling the baby "Nugget," and the nickname caught on. Their outdoor gathering was casual, with seasonal home-cooked food, hard cider, and lots of dogs and children romping about. Guests were greeted with heirloom pumpkins, gourds, and handcrafted garlands, and everyone gathered around a bonfire at evening's end before heading home with little jars of Ashley's homemade cardamom apple butter.

"The most **ecological** choice for food is also the most **ethical** choice for **food**, whether we're **talking** about brussels sprouts or foie gras; and it's also almost always the most **delicious** choice, and that's **serendipitous**."

—philosopher/chef Dan Barber

When Nugget was born, Ashley and Glenn had already decided to name him Huxley, which means "outdoorsman" and "a clearing in the forest." "Our Nugget warming was deeply meaningful for us," explains Ashley. "We wanted to gather everyone together at our home in the woods to enjoy the early autumn harvest and to celebrate where Huxley would live, the meaning of his name, and his birthplace."

Grit Cakes

Serves 6 to 8

- 6 cups water
- 1 tsp. sea salt
- 2 cups stone-ground grits (polenta is the same thing)
- 4 TB. butter
- A few grinds of black pepper
- 3 TB. grated Parmesan

1. Preheat oven to 350°F. Butter a 9 x 13-inch baking dish.

2. In a medium-sized pot over high heat, bring water and salt to a boil. Add grits; reduce heat to low, and cook, stirring occasionally, for 5 minutes.

3. Remove pot from burner. Stir in the butter and a few grinds of pepper. Pour mixture evenly into prepared baking dish. Bake for 25 minutes.

4. Remove grits from oven and sprinkle evenly with Parmesan. Place under broiler until top is golden brown, about 4 minutes. Remove from oven and let cool for about 30 minutes. Place baking dish in refrigerator for 2 hours, or until no longer warm.

5. Use a round cookie cutter to cut out grit cakes; discard the excess. Heat the cakes in a 350°F oven for 20 minutes until hot. Plate and ladle on the topping of your choice.

Gathering at the
DUCK
Shack

Christine Hoffman

Too many cooks in the kitchen? There is no
such thing in Christine Hoffman's family.
Cooking and celebrating together is one of
this family's favorite activities. Every
October, when duck hunting season rolls
around, wild game becomes the focus at the
family cabin. Four generations have enjoyed
gathering at the Duck Shack, as it has been
dubbed, where passions for hunting and
cooking combine in small wild game dinners
or fêtes for up to 200 guests.

The youngest of five siblings, Pies and Aprons blogger Christine Hoffman is treating her family to an intimate dinner featuring their recent catches. Her brothers offer ducks and venison from their bounty, and fall foray pheasants come from her father. As Christine busies herself in the kitchen, family members poke in to do a taste test, offer advice, or grab another cup of coffee. For the most part, everyone is content to enjoy the perfect fall weather around the fire pit, snacking on venison sausage, cheese, and bread before for the main event.

After months of eating fresh-from-the-market salads, Christine loves to sink into the comfort foods of fall. "The colors and tastes of fall ingredients are so stunning," says Christine. "They create such a gorgeous palette for cooking and serving." Brilliantly hued squash and apple rings are roasted, then served over a bed of fresh greens to complement the subtle taste of the apple roasted pheasant. Cranberries, often seen only at the Thanksgiving table, are combined with beets to make a spicy and sweet chutney to serve alongside the roasted ducks. (Continued on page 70.)

Venison Stew

Serves 10 to 12

- 2 TB. olive oil
- 2 medium onions, diced
- 3 lb. venison meat, trimmed and cubed
- 3 cloves garlic, minced
- 1 lb. carrots, peeled and sliced
- 1 bunch celery, sliced
- 6 cups beef broth
- 3 bay leaves
-    Salt and pepper
-    Roasted Tomatoes (see recipe below)
- 3 TB. flour
- ¼ cup warm water

1. Heat olive oil in large saucepan over low heat. Add onions and sauté over medium heat for 2 to 3 minutes. Add venison and garlic and sauté over medium-high heat until meat is browned. Transfer mixture to a stockpot.

2. Add carrots and celery to saucepan and sauté for 8 to 10 minutes. Transfer to stockpot. Add beef broth, bay leaves, and salt and pepper to stockpot. Simmer over medium-low heat for 1 hour.

3. Add roasted tomatoes to stockpot and simmer for 2 hours more.

4. Mix flour into warm water, stirring to dissolve all lumps. Add flour mixture to stew and stir well. Simmer another 20 to 30 minutes, until mixture is thickened and meat is tender.

Roasted Tomatoes

- 2 lb. tomatoes, chopped
- 3 TB. olive oil
- ½ tsp. coarse salt
- ¼ tsp. fresh ground pepper

Preheat oven to 350°F. Combine tomatoes, olive oil, salt, and pepper in a large bowl, stirring to coat tomatoes with oil. Transfer to a 9 x 13-inch glass baking pan. Bake for 1½ hours.

Caramelized Onion and Gruyère Tart

Serves 10 to 12

- 3 TB. olive oil, divided
- 3 large onions, sliced thinly
- 2 TB. butter
- Puff Pastry (see recipe below) or 1 (16- to 18-Oz.) package frozen puff pastry, thawed at room temperature for 40 minutes
- 3 oz. Gruyère, thinly sliced or shaved
- ½ tsp. salt
- ¼ tsp. freshly ground pepper

1. In a large saucepan, heat 2 TB. of the olive oil over low heat. Add onions and butter and sauté over low to medium heat, stirring often, until onions are translucent and golden, 25 to 35 minutes. Do not brown.

2. Preheat oven to 400°F. Roll out puff pastry into a 9 x 12-inch rectangle and place on a baking sheet. Brush with remaining 1 TB. olive oil. Layer onions over pastry. Top with Gruyère. Sprinkle with salt and pepper. Bake for 20 to 25 minutes or until pastry is puffed, cheese is bubbly, and both are lightly browned. Serve warm.

Puff Pastry

- 1½ cups all-purpose flour
- ½ cup cake flour
- ½ tsp. salt
- 1 cup (2 sticks) butter, cut into small pieces
- ½ cup cold water

1. Combine flours, salt, and butter in a large bowl. Cover and place in freezer for 30 minutes.

2. Dump chilled flour mixture into a food processor. Pulse about 10 times. Continuing to pulse, add water in a steady stream until dough comes together in a few clumps. Do not overmix; dough should be lumpy with spots of chunky butter.

3. Turn dough onto a floured surface and press into a rectangle with your hands or a rolling pin. Fold the dough toward you, in half, then roll out again with rolling pin. Repeat folding and rolling motion three times. Shape and flatten dough into a 4 x 12-inch rectangle. Roll it into a tube, wrap in plastic, and refrigerate for 1 hour.

"Be **true** to your work, your **word** and your **friend**."

—Henry David Thoreau

White Bean, Mushroom and Spinach Soup

Serves 8

- 1 medium yellow onion, chopped
- 2 TB. olive oil or butter
- 1 (8-oz.) package white button mushrooms, cleaned and sliced (baby portobellas would be super, too)
- 16 oz. vegetable broth
- 8 oz. frozen spinach (or fresh if you have it)
- 2 tsp. rubbed sage (Rubbed sage is crushed sage, rubbed between the fingers.) or 2 TB. fresh chopped sage
- 2 bay leaves
  Salt and pepper to taste
- 1 (15-oz.) can white beans

1. In a 3-quart stockpot, sauté onion in olive oil or butter for 5 minutes. Add mushrooms and sauté for another 5 minutes.

2. Add broth, bring to boil, and then reduce heat to low. Add spinach, sage, bay leaves, and salt and pepper. Cover and simmer on low heat for 20 minutes.

3. Add white beans and simmer 10 minutes more, or until beans are heated through.

Bean, Corn and Veggie Salad

Serves 4

- 1 (15-oz.) can kidney beans, drained and rinsed
- 1 ear of corn, kernels cut and blanched (I microwaved for 2 minutes)
- 2 carrots, thinly sliced
- ½ cucumber, seeded and thinly sliced (I used my hand mandoline, which I love, love, love!)
- 2 TB. fresh parsley
- 3 TB. olive oil
- 1 TB. red wine vinegar
  Salt and pepper to taste

Throw all of the prepped ingredients into a big bowl and toss well. Serve with fresh guacamole, corn chips, and sliced cheddar. This would also make a good side salad to a main dish of pulled pork or grilled chicken.

Venison stew is a perennial favorite at any wild game meal held at the Duck Shack, but since the Hoffmans are "make it up as you go" cooks, the stew recipe varies from year to year. Roasted tomatoes are Christine's new addition this time around, and they help create a rich and complex base for the stew.

She ladles the stew into brown diner mugs, then loads them onto a rustic metal tray for easy toting to the table. A buttery caramelized onion and Gruyère tart is the perfect accompaniment to the hearty stew. "Store-bought puff pastry is perfectly acceptable," says Christine, "but everyone should try their hand at homemade at least once. It's remarkably easy and really wows with its sinfulness."

Every Friday is "PIE DAY" at Pies and Aprons, so Christine's dessert of choice for this gathering is, naturally, pie. She highlights more seasonal fare with pears in the filling and fresh rosemary in the crust. The two flavors marry perfectly in a just-sweet-enough pie, and the flecks of rosemary make for a beautiful finished product.

In cabin tradition, the dinner bell is rung, signaling those who are taking a walk in the woods or cruising the lake in a duck boat. As everyone gathers at the table, Christine carries in the platters and then allows herself to relax into food, wine, and conversation. Everyone raises a glass to toast yet another festive family meal at the Duck Shack.

Pear Pie with Rosemary Crust

Serves 8

- 2 TB. finely chopped fresh rosemary
-   9-inch double pie crust (store-bought or homemade)
- 6 cups peeled and cubed fresh pears
- 1 cup sugar
- 3 TB. flour
- 2 TB. butter

1. Preheat oven to 350°F. Lightly press rosemary into prepared pie crust (or mix rosemary directly into pastry if making crust from scratch). Line pie plate with bottom crust.

2. Spoon pears into pie shell. Pour sugar over top of pears. Sprinkle flour over the top. Dot with butter. Add top crust and crimp the edges. Pierce holes in top crust to allow steam to escape. Bake for 1 hour 15 minutes or until crust is lightly browned.

71

REMEMBERING MY Mother

A Girlfriends' Garden Party

Patricia Mackey

Patricia Mackey runs a jewelry business called Tippy Stockton. Her love of vintage pieces brought her a new circle of friends that she's grown to rely on even more since her mother's passing. She decided to treat them to a Girlfriends' Garden Party at her home in Edmonds, Washington, a quaint seaside town on the Puget Sound.

73

Patricia Mackey's special women friends came into her life and filled a void after her mother passed away. Her party for them was going to be perfect: A warm summer night with grilled lemon chicken and prawns on the barbecue and a fresh garden salad, accompanied by conversation, laughter, and rich friendship in the garden. She and her girlfriends—a talented photographer, a blessed blogger, a witty shop owner, a vintage doll collector who loves to laugh, and a crafty flea market organizer—all love vintage finds. Their merrymaking would celebrate summer, the Mardi Gras of junking season.

On cue, rain clouds darkened the July skies over the Pacific Northwest the night before their party. Undaunted, Patricia moved the celebration from the garden to the deck. Her husband John helped stretch out the awning, and Patricia hung garden lights all through it. Though she still planned to show her friends her lovely garden studio, she brought plenty of fresh flowers to the table, arranging hydrangeas, roses, and Queen Anne's lace from the garden in vintage aqua glass Ball jars. Dinner would be served buffet style.

"Where **your treasure** is, **your heart** will be also."

—Matthew 6:21

"As I made everything ready for my party," recalls Patricia, "I could almost see the joyous assemblies my mom gathered, with food that never stopped coming out of the oven. My parents weren't wealthy, but my mom could throw a party like nobody's business. No one ever left her table hungry. She loved theme parties, and even after my grandmother, her entertaining accomplice, passed away, my mother continued her perpetual feasts for family and friends."

Though it was a tad chilly, Patricia's garden-party-turned-deck-dinner was everything she anticipated—and maybe more. The conversation ranged from the time she met Ina Garten, The Barefoot Contesssa, on a trip to New York to everyone's attempts to eat gluten-free and healthy. One of the ladies had stopped at a feed store before coming and had purchased two tiny chicks. "We were all intrigued by the little fuzzballs she had in her van," says Patricia, "so she brought them out for us to see. They were absolutely adorable as they waddled around my deck and gardens."

Beauchamp Orchard Salad

Serves 10

- 2 large heads Romaine lettuce, cut into bite-sized pieces
- 1 cup of coarsely chopped Napa cabbage
- 1 apple (Gala in summer, Honeycrisp in Fall) or pear, cut into bite-sized pieces
- 1 (8-oz.) tub of crumbled blue cheese
- Sweet-and-Spicy Pecans (see recipe at right)

For the dressing:

- ½ cup walnut oil
- ¼ cup rice wine vinegar
- 2 TB. minced shallots
- 2 TB. fresh lemon juice
- 2 TB. real maple syrup

1. Combine lettuce, cabbage, apple, and blue cheese in a large bowl.
2. Whisk together walnut oil, vinegar, shallots, lemon juice, and maple syrup. Pour over salad and toss to combine. Top with pecans.

Sweet-and-Spicy Pecans
Makes 4 cups

- 2 (16-oz.) bags of shelled pecans
- ¾ cup sugar
- ¼ tsp. cinnamon
- ¼ tsp. nutmeg
- 2 TB. kosher salt
- ¼ to ½ tsp. cayenne
- 1 egg white
- 1 TB. water

1. Preheat the oven to 225°F.
2. Place pecans in a large bowl. In a separate bowl, mix together sugar, cinnamon, nutmeg, salt, and cayenne.
3. Beat the egg white and water until frothy. Pour egg mixture over pecans and toss to coat. Pour the dry ingredients onto the pecans and toss again until evenly coated. Spread evenly in a roasting pan and bake for 1½ hours. Allow to cool, stirring occasionally so pieces don't clump together. Store at room temperature in an airtight container up to 1 month.

So much laughter and fun. Planning and giving her Girlfriends' Garden Party was a turning point for Patricia. "Somehow," she reflects, "my mother's generosity and can-do heart have passed to me."

Grilled Shrimp

Serves 8 to 10

- 1 medium yellow onion, finely chopped
- 3 garlic cloves, minced
- ¼ cup fresh Italian flat leaf parsley, minced
- ¼ cup fresh basil, minced
- 1 tsp. dry mustard
- 2 TB. Dijon mustard
- 2 tsp. kosher salt
- ¼ tsp. freshly ground pepper
- ¼ cup olive oil
- 1 lemon, juiced
- 2 pounds jumbo shrimp (16 to 20 pieces), peeled and deveined; leave tails on
- 20 wooden skewers

1. Combine onion, garlic, parsley, basil, dry mustard, Dijon mustard, salt, pepper, olive oil, and lemon juice. Toss with shrimp and let marinate for 1 hour or cover and refrigerate for up to 2 days.

2. Soak skewers in water for 20-30 minutes.

3. Lightly grease the grill with cooking oil. Place 2 shrimp on each skewer and grill for 1½ minutes. Flip skewer, and grill for another 1½ minutes.

Grilled Lemon Chicken

Serves 6 to 8

- ¾ cup freshly squeezed lemon juice (about 4 lemons)
- ¾ olive oil
- 2 tsp. kosher salt
- 1 tsp. freshly ground pepper
- 1 TB. fresh thyme leaves, minced or ½ tsp. dried thyme
- 2 pounds boneless chicken breasts, cut diagonally into smaller pieces

1. Whisk together the lemon juice, olive oil, salt, pepper, and thyme. Place chicken in a large Ziploc bag, cover with lemon juice mixture and let marinate for 6 hours in the refrigerator (can do this overnight).

2. Lightly grease the grill with cooking oil. Drain chicken, discarding marinade and grill for 10 minutes per side.

CELEBRATING
the Everyday

Tricia Martin

Tricia Martin is a designer of food experiences that incite interaction, connection, and community. Her projects and events delve into the cultural, societal, historical, and familial aspects of food and eating rituals, and she covers them all in her blog Eating Is Art. Living in the food-loving city of Portland, Oregon, Tricia finds that food is both her medium and her muse; through food, she communicates messages, stories, and ideas.

e for: Apple Kuchen or Purple
he kitchen of: Grandma Martin
cups flour
teaspoon baking powder
teaspoon salt
up sugar
pound butter
cup milk

ft dr

Tricia Martin celebrates the ins and outs of everyday life through food. She is fascinated with the facets of daily life that nourish us and ultimately make us who we are. "Everybody eats," she explains. "Food is the common denominator among all human beings. My focus is on celebrating our commonality, learning from our individuality, and experiencing our stories through the ritual sharing of a meal."

One of Tricia's personal favorite foods is her grandmother's apple kuchen. It is also one of the first things she learned to bake. She remembers scooting up a chair to the counter in order to take the bits of brown sugar her grandmother held out in her large, worn palm. After mixing the batter, her grandmother turned the bowl over to Tricia for some final mixing—"just to make sure I did it right," she'd say with a wink.
(Continued on page 82.)

Apple Kuchen

Serves 8

- 6 large apples of differing varieties (Granny Smith and Honeycrisp work especially well)
- 1 lemon
- 2 cups flour
- 1 tsp. baking powder
- ½ tsp. salt
- ½ cup (1 stick) butter
- 1 cup sugar
- 1 egg
- ½ cup milk

For the topping:

- ½ cup sugar
- ¼ cup flour
- ¼ cup (½ stick) butter
- 1 tsp. cinnamon (my addition to my grandmother's recipe)

1. Preheat oven to 350°F. Butter and flour a 9 x 12-inch baking pan.

2. Peel, core, and slice the apples. Slice a lemon in half and squeeze about 1 TB. juice onto the apples. Toss together. Set aside.

3. Sift together flour, baking powder, and salt. In a mixing bowl, cream butter, sugar, and egg. Add milk and flour mixture alternately, mixing until a smooth batter forms. Spread batter in the prepared pan. Pour the apple slices over the batter, arranging them in a pattern if desired.

4. Using your fingers, combine the sugar, flour, butter, and cinnamon until crumbly. Sprinkle over the apples. Bake for 30 minutes.

"To **communicate** is, in some lexicons, to commune, and that is an **act** more needed now than perhaps ever before on this **planet**."

—M. F. K. Fisher

Almost four years ago, Tricia moved across the country to pursue a master's degree in fine arts and design. After grueling days in the graphic arts studio, she found herself releasing pent-up passion in the kitchen. Pulling out her grandmother's recipes helped heal her disconnect and gave her some needed reassurance. She began asking others for family recipes and through them entered a new world of tasting, remembering, and feeling. Toxic thoughts and poisonous self-doubts—"I can't" and "I'm not good enough"—gave way to exhilarating achievement. She began to see a connection between the foods she ate every day and how she felt about herself. Old wounds could finally heal.

Quinoa Basil and Fresh Corn Salad

Serves 6

- 1½ cups uncooked quinoa, rinsed well
- 1 tsp. salt
- 3 cups water
- 2 cups corn, fresh (from about 4 ears) or frozen
- 1 cup tightly packed basil leaves, finely chopped
- ½ cup sliced sun-dried tomatoes (soaked in hot water for 15 minutes before slicing)
- ½ cup diced red onion
- 2 TB. olive oil
- 1 or 2 lemons, juiced (3 to 5 TB.)

1. In a medium saucepan, combine quinoa, salt, and 3 cups water. Bring to a boil over high heat. Cover, reduce heat to low, and simmer 12 minutes.

2. Add corn to quinoa. Cover and cook until quinoa is tender but still a little crunchy, about 3 minutes. Drain well, transfer to large serving bowl, and toss with a fork to fluff and separate the quinoa grains. Set aside to cool slightly.

3. Add basil, sun-dried tomatoes, and onion. Stir in oil and enough lemon juice to give salad a distinct lemony edge. Adjust seasonings to taste and serve.

Morning Oats

Serves 2 to 3

- 1 cup steel-cut oats
- 2 cups filtered water
- 1 apple
- 3 TB. freshly ground flax seeds
  Real maple syrup
  Pinch of cinnamon (optional)

1. Rinse the steel-cut oats and place in a large pot. Add the water and bring to a boil. Reduce heat to low, cover, and cook for 30 minutes.

2. Spoon cooked oatmeal into a deep bowl. Grate the apple with a box grater and add to bowl. Add flax seeds and pour a liberal amount of real maple syrup on top. If feeling spicy, add a pinch of cinnamon.

Tricia was curious to see if others related to food in the same way, and she began creating eating experiences where people could connect and communicate. Called "Eating Design," her work explores the timeless language of food and the ways that food is a catalyst and a connector on a very basic human level. What other language lets you learn about other people and cultures without actually speaking?

Knowing how to eat what you need, is, Tricia feels, the quintessential challenge of being human. She wasn't worried about calories or fat content; her focus was "tasting" the stories behind different foods and feeding her soul. Subconsciously, she gravitated towards whole foods, grains, and produce. She experimented with spices and tried new varieties of vegetables and fruits. The sheer vastness of the edible world called out to her. Conscious of her eating, Tricia concluded that eating is an art. Practicing that art is a way of caring for oneself, body and soul, day in and day out.

Along with celebrating the everyday, Tricia loves the weddings, reunions, and other "big" celebrations that come with her work as an event designer. They offer her a daily opportunity to throw a spotlight on ordinary pleasures and help others experience them through the sensation of the spectacular. The result is a rich and textured tapestry where the small pleasures of life end up making all the difference.

a Life filled with Spice

An Evening of Moroccan Memories

Helene Dujardin

If there were a recipe for making friends, French-born Marie-Helene Dujardin of Charleston, South Carolina, could have invented it. Author of the award-winning food blog, Tartelette, and professional photographer and food stylist, Helene has the talent and style to see beauty in all things. She credits this ability to her beloved grandmother, Paulette, and honors her memory by creating her grandmother's infamous couscous dish for an outdoor gathering by the water with friends.

"My full, real, baptized name is Marie-Helene, but computers in the states don't seem to get the hyphens right and keep cutting my name in half," says Helene with her lovely French accent. Both of her parents were born in Morocco, but they met in France, where Helene was born. Her mother's parents were French, but they were stationed for a while in Morocco during World War II. Helene was devoted to her grandmother, Paulette, who was "always in the kitchen. She was the glue in our family. When it came to food, her attitude was that there will be enough for all."

Helene's party is a simple gathering with friends near the water at her home. Sawhorses and planks of wood serve as tables. Tablecloths thrown over the top look chic in an effortless French sort of way. With a sense of community her grandmother would recognize, everyone pitches in. John Ondo, the chef at Lana's Restaurant, supplied the silverware, linens, platters, dishes, and hard-to-find spicy lamb sausage. Fanny and Patrick Panella, owners of Bin 152 wine bar, the group's rendezvous for the past year, provided the wine and helped set up the dinner party. "I just let them come in and start helping, as I finish the cooking. Whatever they do is perfect," says Helene.

Moroccan Couscous

(also known as Couscous Berbere)

Serves 10 to 12

- 6 TB. olive oil, divided
- 1 small chicken, cut up
- 2 lb. lamb shoulder, cut into 1-inch chunks
- 3 medium onions, cut into large chunks
- 2 TB. Ras-El-Hanout spice blend* (recipe follows)
- 4 carrots, cut into large chunks
- 4 medium tomatoes or 1 (14-oz.) can diced tomatoes
- 3 turnips, cut into medium dice
- 4 zucchini, cut into large chunks
  Salt and pepper
- 2 (10-oz.) boxes plain dry couscous**
- 1 (14-oz.) can chickpeas, drained and rinsed
- ½ cup golden raisins
- ¼ cup to ⅓ cup Harissa paste***

*For this recipe, start by using 2 TB. of spice blend. See how you like it and how strong it tastes to you and adjust by adding a bit more if desired.

**Brown rice couscous can be substituted to keep this dish entirely gluten-free.

***Harissa is a strong chili paste from North Africa that can be found easily online or in specialty shops. It is very strong, so use with caution.

1. In a large Dutch oven or stockpot, heat 2 TB. of the olive oil over medium heat. Add chicken pieces and sauté until golden brown. Remove from the pot and set aside.

2. Add another 2 TB. of olive oil to the pot, add lamb chunks, and sauté to a nice brown color on the outside. Remove from the pot and set aside.

3. In the same pot, heat the remaining 2 TB. of olive oil, add the onions, and sauté until golden brown. Add the lamb and chicken back into the pot, the Ras-El-Hanout, and enough water to cover. Bring to a boil, reduce the heat to a simmer, and cook for about 1 hour.

4. Add the carrots, tomatoes, and turnips and cook for another 30 minutes. Add the zucchini last and cook for another 30 minutes. Adjust the seasoning with salt and pepper and more Ras-El-Hanout if needed.

5. Prepare the couscous according to package directions (Helene steams the couscous while the meat cooks). Add the chickpeas and raisins to the couscous and mix well.

6. Dissolve the Harissa paste into ½ cup of the cooking liquid from the meat, stirring with a spoon. Either pour some to taste (it's quite hot) into the couscous or serve it on the side for guests to add according to their taste for spiciness. To serve, scoop some couscous into a large bowl and top with chicken, lamb, vegetables, and plenty of broth.

Ras-El-Hanout Spice Blend

- 1 tsp. ground cumin
- 1 tsp. ground ginger
- 1 tsp. tumeric
- 1 tsp. salt
- ¾ tsp. ground cinnamon
- ¾ tsp. freshly ground black pepper
- ½ tsp. ground white pepper
- ½ tsp. ground coriander seeds
- ½ tsp. cayenne
- ½ tsp. ground allspice
- ½ tsp. ground nutmeg
- ¼ tsp. ground cloves

Combine all the ingredients in a small bowl. Sieve at least once before using.

"The Ras–El–Hanout spice blend is nothing to put together. Even if the list of ingredients is long, most of these spices are probably already in your pantry. It keeps well and can be used on grilled meats and fish as well as a seasoning for vegetables."

The group gathers around the table at high tide. Helene serves the couscous in the traditional way, topping it with savory meats and vegetables that have stewed for hours and become very tender. Harissa, a chili paste, is served in little bowls so that guests may spice their dishes as they like. Helene tells the story of how her grandmother, Paulette, the prankster of the family, would sneak up and dump an entire bowl of Harissa into the couscous, spicing it up to the point that everyone would be crying (and laughing) from the heat. "The heat never bothered her at all," laughs Helene.

Paulette passed away five years ago, but Helene's grandfather, Rene, is still alive at 100 years old. When Helene made a comment to him about slowing down, he boisterously replied, "I'm starting my second century! I've got things to do!" It is easy to see that the Moroccan influence in Helene's family roots runs deep with love and energy, the true spices of life.

"This is **me**, and I'm **cool** with me, and if you're not cool with me, **well** then, that's **you**."

—my friend Karen Walrond, author of *The Beauty of Different*

Honey and Saffron Ice Cream

Makes 3 cups

  2 cups heavy cream
  1 cup whole milk
  ½ cup wildflower honey
    Pinch of saffron

1. In a large saucepan, stir together the cream, milk, and honey. Bring the mixture to a simmer over medium-low heat, stirring occasionally to blend. Remove from the heat and allow to steep. Cool to room temperature and refrigerate, preferably overnight, until the honey is infused.

2. To prepare the ice cream, add a few threads of saffron and stir. Process the mixture in an ice cream maker according to the manufacturer's instructions.

Cardamom Cookies

Makes 18 to 20 cookies

  ½ cup (1 stick) unsalted butter, at room temperature
  ¾ cup confectioners' sugar
  1 large egg
  ½ cup millet flour
  ½ cup sweet rice flour
  ½ cup potato starch
  2 TB. cornstarch
  ½ tsp. ground cardamom
    Pinch of salt

1. In a mixer, cream the butter and sugar together until light and fluffy. Add the egg and mix until combined.

2. Add the millet and sweet rice flours, the potato starch and cornstarch, and the cardamom and salt. Mix briefly to incorporate. Dump the mixture onto a lightly floured board and gather the dough into a smooth ball. Flatten the dough into a disk, wrap it in plastic wrap, and refrigerate for 1 hour.

3. Position a rack in the middle of the oven. Preheat the oven to 350°F. Roll out the chilled dough between sheets of parchment paper or plastic wrap to a ¼-inch thickness. Cut out cookies with a 3-inch round cookie cutter. Place cookies on a baking sheet lined with parchment paper or a non-stick baking mat. Bake for 8 to 10 minutes. Cool in pan or on wire racks.

Tenth Anniversary

An Oktoberfest Celebration

Andrea Meyers

Andrea is a wife and mother to three boys living in Loudoun County in Northern Virginia. She grew up on the good Southern cooking of her mother and grandmothers, then later learned to love food from all over the world when she spent eight years teaching abroad and traveling in 23 countries. Her cooking is influenced by travel and the fresh produce from their garden, and each year she and her husband celebrate their anniversary with a German meal inspired by their Oktoberfest honeymoon.

Andrea Meyers has always connected food to the places she has lived and visited, and to the special moments in her life. Her childhood in Virginia was filled with the aromas and tastes of fried chicken, country ham, biscuits and gravy, apple butter, and coconut cake. Those memories melded with others when she accepted her first teaching job overseas.

Andrea first dreamed of traveling to Germany while studying the language in high school. She traveled there in 1996 with a tour group and had her first German *brezel* (pretzel), *schnitzel* (a seasoned and garnished veal cutlet), and *spätzle* (German noodles). Andrea's husband was interested in Germany's festive culture, and his dream, since college, was to participate in a Munich Oktoberfest. As they planned their autumn wedding in Bar Harbour, Maine, Michael and Andrea quickly latched onto the idea of honeymooning in Germany and attending Oktoberfest, which began as a wedding celebration in 1810. (Continued on page 94.)

Whole Wheat Spätzle (German Noodles)

Serves 4

German noodles, or *spätzle*, are very easy to make at home using a round press-style potato ricer. The thick batter is pressed through the ricer into boiling water. Most ricers come with two discs, one with large holes and the other with small holes; the larger holes produce the better noodle. Andrea says "We started adding whole wheat pastry flour to our spätzle, which gives it more nutritional value and a slightly nutty flavor. We've also tried all-whole-wheat flour, but settled on this version for the texture."

- ¾ cup whole wheat flour
- ¾ cup unbleached all-purpose flour
- ½ tsp. ground nutmeg
- 1¼ tsp. salt, divided
- ⅛ tsp. pepper
- 3 eggs
- 3 ozs. lowfat milk

1. In a small bowl, whisk together the whole wheat pastry flour, all-purpose flour, nutmeg, ¾ tsp. of the salt, and pepper.

2. Beat the eggs in the medium bowl. Add half the milk and half of the flour mixture and stir. Add the remaining milk and flour mixture and stir until smooth. Let the batter rest for 30 minutes.

3. In a 4-quart pot, bring water to boil and add remaining ½ tsp. salt. Press the batter through the ricer or spätzle press, into the water. When the spätzle floats to the top of the water, drain well with a large slotted spoon and transfer it to a bowl. Serve spätzle hot with butter, with cheese and onions (*käsespätzle*), or with meat dishes with sauces such as *sauerbraten* and *jägerschnitzel*.

German-Style Green Beans

Serves 4

The flavor in this dish comes from bacon, which is sautéed and added to the steamed beans along with a portion of the drippings. Steaming retains nutrients and keeps the beans from turning mushy.

- 1 lb. fresh green beans, trimmed and cut into 2-inch pieces
- 4 bacon strips, diced
- 1 large onion, chopped
- ⅛ tsp. freshly ground black pepper
- Salt

1. Place a steamer basket in the bottom of a large pot and add about 1 inch of water. Add the green beans, cover the pot, and bring to a boil. Reduce heat to medium and cook until just tender, 3 to 5 minutes.

2. While the beans steam, cook the bacon strips in a large skillet over medium-high heat until they just start to get crispy. Add the onions and sauté until they are tender, about 3 minutes.

3. Drain the beans and return them to the pot. Add the cooked onions and a little of the bacon drippings. Crumble the bacon and toss with the beans. Add pepper and salt to taste. Serve hot.

Their wedding trip became a quest to taste as much of the German wine, beer, and food as they could in 11 days. Each town they visited in the Rhine region played its own theme of the four basic ingredients that make beer, and they landed in Munich on the opening day of Oktoberfest. "Chilly and wet, we spent the day wandering about the beer tents and eating *brezels* and brats and drinking good German beer. I'm amazed that I didn't look like a brat after that trip because I think I tasted nearly every kind of sausage made in the country and ate my share of pretzels and washed it all down with beer and wine. Our thoughts on beer changed dramatically during that trip, and we haven't looked at beer in the same way since."

Black Forest Cake

Every year on their wedding anniversary, Andrea and Michael have a little German party in honor of their honeymoon in Germany and excursion to Oktoberfest. They drink German wine and beer and make their favorite German foods while oompah band tunes and other Oktoberfest music plays in the background. "In 2010 we celebrated our tenth anniversary over a whole weekend," says Andrea. "For one meal we had grilled brats with sauerkraut and *kartoffelsalat* (potato salad), and for another we had schnitzel, *spätzle*, and German-style green beans." Their boys were very excited about eating *laugenbrotchen* (pretzel rolls), though some years they make regular pretzels. Of course, everyone in the family loves seeing and eating the pretty Black Forest Cake. Ever since their first son arrived eight years ago, Andrea and Michael have always included their children in the anniversary meal as a way of celebrating not only their years as a couple but the family they've created.

"Don't **play** as if you've **swallowed** the metronome."

—Nadia Boulanger, French composer, teacher, and conductor, 1887-1979

Jägerschnitzel
(Pork Schnitzel with Creamy Mushroom Sauce)
Serves 4

Schnitzel is a meat dish, usually veal or pork or chicken, in which the meat has been pounded thin. Breading and frying the meat is a style attributed to Vienna, Austria, hence the name *Wiener schnitzel*. The word *jäger* means "hunter" in German and refers to the creamy sauce that accompanies the fried meat. This autumn and winter comfort food goes perfectly with the German spätzle, or noodles.

- 4 pork cutlets or thin-cut pork chops, pounded thin to about ½-inch thick
- Salt
- Freshly ground black pepper
- ¼ cup unbleached all-purpose flour
- 3 eggs, beaten
- ⅓ cup fine dry bread crumbs
- 4 TB. sunflower oil or olive oil
- 4 slices thick-cut bacon, chopped
- 1 onion, chopped
- 8 ozs. sliced mushrooms, chopped
- 2 TB. minced fresh parsley leaves
- ½ cup Pinot Noir
- 2 cups heavy whipping cream

1. Season the meat with salt and pepper. Dredge the pieces in the flour and shake off excess. Dip the pieces in the egg and allow the excess to drip off, then dredge in the bread crumbs until fully coated.

2. In a large, heavy sauté pan, heat the oil over high heat. Add the meat and sear until golden on both sides. Move the meat to a platter lined with paper towels and cover with another paper towel.

3. Add the bacon to the pan and cook over medium-high heat until the bacon starts to brown, 3 to 5 minutes. Add the onions and cook while stirring until onions soften and begin to glisten, about 2 minutes. Add the mushrooms and cook while stirring until mushrooms soften, about 3 minutes. Add the parsley and cook for 1 minute more.

4. Deglaze the pan with the wine, stirring while cooking until it reduces, about 5 minutes. Add the whipping cream and bring to a boil, then reduce heat and simmer until it thickens, about 5 minutes. Place the schnitzel on plates with spätzle (recipe on page 92), then spoon the mushroom sauce over all and serve.

95

Laugenbrötchen (German Pretzel Rolls)

Makes 8 rolls

German pretzels and pretzel rolls are dark and crusty on the outside and chewy on the inside. Traditional recipes call for the rolls to take a little lye bath before going into the oven. Because food grade lye is not widely available, baking soda makes a good substitute.

3¾ cups unbleached bread flour

2¼ tsp. instant yeast (aka bread machine yeast)

2 TB. salt

1 TB. granulated sugar

1 cup plus 2 TB. warm water, 110°F–115°F

Canola oil, for coating the rising bowl

Course salt, for sprinkling on top

For the boiling mixture:

8 cups water

½ cup baking soda

1. In the bowl of a stand mixer, whisk together the flour, yeast, salt, and sugar. Make a well in the middle and pour in 1 cup of the warm water. Stir by hand until the dough starts to come together. If the dough is a little dry, add another 1 to 2 TB. of warm water and stir it in; if it's wet, add another 1 to 2 TB. of flour. Put the bowl on the stand mixer and knead with the dough hook on medium speed until the dough is smooth and elastic and cleans the sides of the bowl, about 4 to 5 minutes. The dough will be stiff.

2. Turn the dough out and shape it into a ball. Put it in the bottom of a large mixing bowl lightly coated with canola oil and rub the surface of the dough lightly with a little more oil. Cover with plastic wrap and set in a warm place. Allow to rise until doubled, about 1½ to 2 hours.

3. Preheat the oven to 400°F. Line a baking sheet with parchment paper and coat lightly with cooking spray.

4. Divide the risen dough into eight equal pieces. Take one ball and turn it around in your hands, stretching the top of the dough and tucking the bottom under. Place the roll on a wooden board or silicone mat and roll it around until it has a round shape. Repeat with the remaining pieces of dough.

5. In a 3-quart pot, bring the water and baking soda to a boil. Using a large wire strainer spoon, insert each roll carefully into the boiling solution for about 10 to 15 seconds. Lift out, allowing the water to drain off. Place the roll on the prepared baking sheet. Repeat for the remaining rolls. Use a serrated knife or razor blade to slash a cross in top of each roll. Sprinkle on the coarse salt.

6. Bake in the preheated oven until the rolls are dark brown, 15 to 20 minutes. Transfer rolls to a wire rack to cool. Best when eaten within one day.

PICKING Pumpkin Party

Celebrating Fall the Old-fashioned Way

Jaime Mormann-Richardson

As a food stylist, photographer, and blogger, Jaime Mormann-Richardson is constantly in the kitchen. But when it comes to celebrations with her own children, she tries to slow down the pace and enjoy the moment to the fullest. She turned a fall excursion to the pumpkin patch near her home in Provo, Utah, into a memorable day.

Jaime Mormann-Richardson loves to celebrate. "It's not like my house explodes with knickknacks every Easter or anything." She says it's more about slowing things down. Her favorite holidays are celebrated best with unhurried family traditions, in thinking, talking, savoring, and cooking.

This is when she likes to invite the kids to help, or at least watch. "It's different when I'm working, trying to get something to look perfect in a photograph. But on our down time, if my kids are standing in my space and I get stressed out, then I know I'm taking things too seriously."

Of all the seasons of the year, fall is Jaime's favorite. The appearance of pumpkins and crunchy leaves seems to signal all the holiday celebrations to come. "Whenever I smell frost in the air mixed with burning wood, I get a chill, and suddenly I'm a child again, giddy about Christmas, even though it's still months away."

Pumpkin Doughnuts with Maple Butter Glaze

Makes 1 dozen

- 1 package instant yeast
- 1 cup warm (110°F) water
- 2 TB. sugar
- 8 TB. butter, melted, divided
- 7 TB. pure maple syrup, divided
- ½ cup canned pumpkin purée
- 2 eggs
- 4 to 5 cups all-purpose flour, divided
- 1 tsp. ground cinnamon
- ½ tsp. ground nutmeg
- 1 tsp. salt
- 8 cups vegetable oil
- 1½ cups confectioners' sugar
- 1 to 2 TB. heavy cream or bottled eggnog

1. Mix yeast and water with sugar in the bowl of an electric mixer fitted with the paddle attachment. Let sit for several minutes until the yeast begins to bubble. Add 4 TB. of the melted butter, 4 TB. of the maple syrup, pumpkin, and eggs. Mix until just combined.

2. With the mixer on low speed, add 2 cups of the flour, cinnamon, nutmeg, and salt. Mix until incorporated. Add as much of the remaining flour as necessary to make a smooth, sticky dough. Switch to the dough hook, and knead for 10 minutes. Transfer to an oiled bowl, cover, and let rise for 1 to 2 hours, or until doubled in bulk.

3. Punch down dough and roll out to a ¼-inch thickness on a slightly oiled surface. Cut out dough with a 5-inch round cookie cutter and cut the center with a 1-inch round cookie cutter. Let doughnuts rest on an oiled baking dish. Heat oil in a heavy-bottomed pot until it reaches 350°F. Fry one to four doughnuts at a time (as many as will fit comfortably in the pot without crowding), a minute or two on each side, until golden brown. Transfer to a cooling rack to drain.

4. For glaze, whisk together confectioners' sugar with remaining 4 TB. butter and 3 TB. maple syrup. Whisk in cream or eggnog to achieve a thick yet runny consistency. Dip warm doughnuts in glaze and set on a rack to cool.

Jaime feels it's important to create special moments with her children. "We need celebrations to bind us closer, make us more unified and strong—we need that strength of family more than we ever did before." Since moving with her children to a basement apartment, Jaime misses her large, sun-filled kitchen, but she simply brings the fun outdoors.

The Pumpkin Picking Party starts in the car, as her three kids, ages 10, 7, and 4, try their best to not quibble on the drive to the pumpkin farm. When they arrive, they find plenty to do and see, from a hayride, to a petting zoo, to a straw maze and a pool of dried corn kernels to play in. They take their time enjoying the attractions, and everyone picks a pumpkin from the patch.

Back at home, the pumpkins are arranged on the front step, and Jaime and her children enter a house filled with the aroma of hearty beef stew. The stew has been simmering in a slow cooker since the previous night and is ready to eat. For an after-supper snack, Jaime and her daughter cut doughnuts from a yeasted pumpkin dough made the night before, fry them in oil, and drizzle warm maple butter glaze over the top. Jaime serves them with cool cider for those who want to keep things light and autumn spice white hot chocolate for those who want something rich and warm.

"The idea of this celebration," Jaime notes, "is to create a sunshiny image my children can hold onto for the rest of their lives. Life isn't always pleasant, but if I can give them a few perfect afternoons like this, then later in life, when they look back and string together all their memories, they'll see happy moments as well as difficult ones. I hope they see a completed necklace that is beautiful because their lives have been full."

Slow Cooker Beef Stew

Serves 8

- 2 lb. stew meat, or 2 lb. chuck roast, cut into 1-inch pieces
- 4 TB. olive oil, divided
  Salt and pepper
- 1 onion, finely chopped
- 1 cup 100% grape juice
- 1 TB. balsamic vinegar
- 1 tsp. dried thyme leaves
- 2 tsp. finely chopped fresh rosemary, plus sprigs for garnish
- 1½ lb. carrots, peeled and chopped
- 3 large potatoes, unpeeled, cut in 1-inch pieces
- 1 large rutabaga, peeled and chopped in ½-inch pieces
- 1 (15-oz.) can tomato purée
- 4 cups chicken stock

1. Toss the stew meat with 3 TB. of the olive oil and a pinch of salt and pepper. Working in small batches, brown the meat in a skillet over medium-high heat and transfer to the slow cooker.

2. Add the remaining 1 TB. olive oil to the skillet. Add the onion and stir to deglaze the pan. Pour in the grape juice and vinegar. Add the onion mixture to the slow cooker.

3. Add the thyme, rosemary, carrots, potatoes, rutabaga, tomato purée, and chicken stock to slow cooker. Cook on low for 8 hours or overnight. Taste and adjust seasonings before serving.

Celebrations
Moroccan
Style
at Peacock Pavilions

Maryam Montague

Maryam Montague gave up any plans she may have had for a white picket fence in suburbia and moved to an olive grove in Marrakech, Morocco, in 2006. At Peacock Pavilions, her home and a boutique hotel, she creates celebrations big and small. Her parties are chronicled on her blog, My Marrakesh (*www.mymarrakesh.com*). Maryam's illustrated lifestyle book will be published in the United States by Artisan Books in 2012.

Her love of food, her love of entertaining, started—as many things do—at the beginning. And at the beginning there was her mother. Now, her mother wasn't like the other mothers in the New York suburbs where she grew up. First of all, she was from Iran, and she had a long glossy sweep of black hair that fell to her waist. Second of all, she knew exotic recipes by heart that confounded all the neighbors. Her mother was part of the slow food movement even before there was a slow food movement, tenderly soaking and simmering rice "the long way," grinding walnuts multiple times for rich sauces, and making light-as-air cookies from an old-fashioned, lacy Iranian cookie press. Her kitchen was heady with the scents of parsley and saffron.

But as much as she enjoyed cooking for her family, my mother loved entertaining for a crowd even more. Her specialty was the cocktail party, and our household would pitch in with a kind of dedication that even Martha Stewart would approve. While I would sauté whole mushroom caps in butter, my mother would spread caviar—smuggled in handbags from Iran—on circles of white bread pressed out with a tea glass. We would then fervently arrange flowers picked from the garden and slim branches cut from our back woods, mixing them with herbs and blooms bought at the supermarket. My mother also believed in dressing the part for her parties and had a wardrobe of jaw-dropping dresses and skirts in saturated colors and patterns that swished right to the floor. When the guests finally arrived, everything would be ready: music playing, drinks served, canapés passed, and my mother—a bright star in the room—mingling. She was the most glamorous woman that I knew.

(Continued on page 106.)

Peacock Pavilions Black Olive Bread with Rosemary

Makes 18 to 20 rolls or small baguettes

- 4 cups wheat flour, sifted, plus more for coating
- 4 cups all-purpose white flour, sifted
- 1 TB. dry yeast
- 4½ tsp. salt
- 1 cup black olives (or more, to your taste), pitted and roughly chopped

  Fresh rosemary, cleaned and very finely chopped, about ¼ cup (or more, to your taste)
- 1½ cups warm water

1. Sift the flours together onto a clean, dry countertop and make a large well at the center. Add the yeast, salt, chopped olives, and chopped rosemary to the center of the well. Add the warm water gradually in small batches to the center of the well and knead. All the ingredients should be well combined and the dough slightly firm. Let the kneaded dough rest for 5 to 10 minutes.

2. Sprinkle about 1 cup of whole wheat flour over work surface. Break off small amounts of dough and roll into small balls or baguettes. Coat each dough ball or baguette with extra whole wheat flour and flatten it slightly in your hands. Use a knife to make a few crosses on the top, for decoration, if desired.

3. Place dough on an ungreased baking pan, cover, and place in a warm area. Let the dough rise for 30 minutes to an hour. Bake in a preheated 320°F oven for 30 to 40 minutes, or until rolls/baguettes are golden brown.

Given all that, it was no surprise that I grew up wanting to be just like my mother. And I still do. Now, of course, I've managed to blaze my own path. And so, after a trip or two around the globe, my American architect husband, our two children, and I settled down, not in New York, but in Marrakech, right in the middle of an olive grove. And it is here that we designed and built the house and boutique hotel that are collectively known as Peacock Pavilions, named after the fanciful pets that roam our garden.

It is in the kitchen of Peacock Pavilions that I try to re-create some of the cooking magic that I grew up with, albeit with a Moroccan flair. Morocco has an extensive tradition of cuisine and at its heart is the *tagine*—a slow-cooked meal served in a conical clay dish by the same name. Tagines come in many varieties (chicken with preserved lemon, lamb with almonds, meatballs in a savory tomato sauce, to name just a few). On Fridays there is couscous, heaped with vegetables and a choice of chicken, beef, or lamb and topped with carmelized onions. Almond stuffed cookies abound, and bread is made fresh daily. All of those traditions have become our own at Peacock Pavilions, with a few twists, such as the abundant inclusion of olives and rosemary in dishes.

Living in our own olive grove with rosemary hedges comes in handy. But although good food is at the heart of every delicious meal, an inspired setting is also important. With the help of Melanie Royals of Royal Design Studio, we designed our very own special Moroccan dining tent. The tent features Moroccan embroidery patterns painted in black against ivory, an ever-chic color and pattern combination. It is in the tent that we host dinners that we hope will surprise and enchant our guests. How often do you get to eat in a tent, after all?
(Continued on page 108.)

Peacock Pavilions Moroccan Chicken Tagine with Olives and Preserved Lemon

Serves 4

- 1 whole chicken
- 1 cup olive oil, divided
- 3 cloves garlic, minced
    Small bunches of coriander and parsley, chopped
- 2 yellow onions, chopped
- 1 preserved lemon
    Pinch of saffron
- 1 tsp. salt
- 1 tsp. pepper
- 3 tsp. cinnamon
- 1 cup green olives

1. Clean and cut up the chicken into large pieces and peel off the skin. Heat 2 TB. of the olive oil in a frying pan, add the chicken, and fry quickly until lightly colored, approximately 2 minutes.

2. Mix garlic, coriander, and parsley. Put a Moroccan tagine (or a large skillet with a lid) on a burner over low heat and add 2 TB. of the oil. Transfer the chicken to the tagine. Sprinkle the garlic-and-herb mixture over the chicken. Add the onions.

3. Rinse the preserved lemon in water and cut it in half. Use a spoon to scoop out and spread the inside pulp over the top of the chicken pieces. Cut the lemon rind into slices and add to the tagine. Add the saffron, salt and pepper, cinnamon, and remaining ¾ cup oil. Cover and cook on medium heat for 1 hour (or for 30 minutes if cooking in a skillet). Add green olives 5 minutes before serving.

"And above all, **watch** with **glittering** eyes the whole **world** around **you** because the greatest secrets are always **hidden** in the most unlikely **places**. Those who don't believe in **magic** will never **find** it."

—Roald Dahl

Peacock Pavilions
Simply Spiced Oranges

Serves 4

> 4 ripe navel oranges
> 1 tsp. granulated sugar, or to taste
> ½ tsp. cinnamon, or to taste

1. Peel oranges, making sure that inner white pith is thoroughly removed. Slice into ⅛- to ¼-inch rounds.

2. Arrange orange rounds on a plate in concentric circles. Sprinkle granulated sugar over the oranges. Top off with cinnamon and serve with a flourish!

We host creative retreats at Peacock Pavilions (painting, writing, photography, decorating, yoga, etc.) and want to make sure that our guests unwind in style after a day of learning or paying visits to the Marrakech souks. So on any given evening, we will be whipping up Moroccan meals in the Peacock Pavilions kitchen and creating dinner party ambiance in the Moroccan tent. That was the case when Holly Becker and Angela Ritchie organized a Moroccan interior design and blogging retreat at Peacock Pavilions (this is their group on page 103). The result? Small-scale celebrations to remember!

a MIDWEEK Get-Together

Shea Fragoso
Debbie Murray

Shea Fragoso and Debbie Murray are the mother-daughter team behind "A Gilded Life." They live and work in a renovated gothic church in Dallas, Texas, where Shea loves nothing more than to plan a celebration. She has an abiding love for entertaining her friends and family, and she is always looking forward to the next "special occasion."

Shea Fragoso is a hopeless romantic and a born hostess. Growing up, even her childhood tea parties were extravagant and elaborately decorated affairs. "I love nothing more than being surrounded by beautiful things, wonderful food, and inspiring people," says Shea. "Bringing friends and family together, whether in small, intimate gatherings or large-scale soirées, has always been a source of profound joy for me, and I am always looking for a good reason to throw a party!"

At home, Shea is blessed with a large, comfortable kitchen, custom-built for her by her father, who truly understands her love of entertaining. He handcrafted a space that is the perfect welcoming spot to gather dear friends and family together for great food and lively conversation. Shea's kitchen is the absolute heart of her home. She has hosted more parties and small gatherings in the two years she has lived there than she can remember!

Even though her business life has given Shea amazing opportunities to plan and host large-scale parties, weddings, and fund-raisers, one of her favorite ways to personally entertain is to gather a handful of girlfriends together for a casual evening of simple, delicious food and drink. These impromptu dinners are a welcome break in the midst of hectic lives, and they provide a chance for Shea and her friends to catch up with each other in a relaxing, comforting atmosphere.

Guacamole

Serves 6 to 8

    3   avocados, peeled and cubed
        Juice of 1 lime
    ½   tsp. salt
        Pinch of black pepper
    ¼   tsp. cayenne (optional)
    ¼   tsp. cumin (optional)
    ½   cup diced onion
    2   Roma (plum) tomatoes, diced and seeded
    3   TB. chopped cilantro
    1   clove garlic, minced

1. In a large bowl toss the cubed avocado with the lime juice to coat.

2. Add the salt and pepper. Add the cumin and cayenne, if using. Mash avocado with a fork or potato masher.

3. Add the onions, tomatoes, cilantro, and garlic. Let sit at room temperature for 1 hour before serving.

To simplify the preparations for a midweek get-together, Shea takes advantage of great prepared food and then adds in her own homemade sides and "a wonderful drink recipe." In the case of this casual dinner, given in honor of visiting friends, she went to her favorite Latin market and bought marinated chicken and fajita beef, Spanish rice, and refried beans. The market also sells lovely grilled onions and handmade corn and flour tortillas. Once these were brought home, Shea and her mother, Debbie Murray, just needed to grill the meat and heat the tortillas. They made fresh guacamole, salsa, and a large batch of their favorite sangria. To end the meal, a simple fresh fruit tray is always perfect!

For Shea, fresh flowers are an absolute must to liven any party décor, and they always make guests feel special and cared for. The grocery store is a great resource for simple, beautiful blooms. Roses and hydrangeas are at the top of Shea's list, and she loves the casual elegance and effortless chic of using all white.
(Continued on page 115.)

"The **grand** essentials of happiness are: something to do, something to **love**, and something to **hope** for."

—Allan K. Chalmers

Sangria

Serves 6 to 8

½ cup brandy

¼ cup lemon juice

⅓ cup frozen lemonade concentrate

⅓ cup orange juice

1 (750 ml) bottle dry red wine

½ cup Triple Sec

¼ cup white sugar (optional)

1 lemon, sliced into rounds

1 lime, sliced into rounds

1 grapefruit, sliced into rounds

1 orange, sliced into rounds

1 peach, cut into 1-inch pieces

2 cups club soda (optional)

1. In a large pitcher or bowl, mix together the brandy, lemon juice, lemonade concentrate, orange juice, red wine, Triple Sec, and sugar, if using.

2. Float slices of lemon, lime, grapefruit, orange, and peach in the mixture. Refrigerate overnight for best flavor.

3. For a fizzy sangria, add club soda just before serving.

One rule Shea was taught early on, and that she truly lives by every time she entertains, is to always use the good china, the beautiful glasses, the most precious serving pieces. "Don't save them for a 'special' occasion. There is nothing more special than a lovely meal with friends and family, even in the middle of the week!"

The **Birthday Club**

Gal Pal Gluten-Free Luncheon

Jen O'Connor

Jen O'Connor is the founder of *www.earthangelstoys.com* which is both an online art gallery and a traveling art show representing the top artists in their fields. Jen is also a contributing editor to several artful lifestyle and décor magazines. She loves to cook and, perhaps even more, to entertain. She maintains busy work and family schedules, especially in the spring when she travels to numerous events and folk art shows, so she offered to host her gal pals' spring gathering to assure her chance of seeing them. Finding a few hours in their busy schedules is always a challenge but well worth the effort; a festive luncheon adds a sweetness to their day and buoys their spirits.

They call themselves "The Birthday Club." Sometimes there is actually a birthday at hand, but more often, the group simply gathers to celebrate one another and to reconnect. These women met years ago when their children were in preschool together, and they all agree: If you don't make the time to gather and catch up a bit, the weeks can slip away into months, and time just passes much too quickly!

For her Birthday Club, the friends gathered at the home of Jen O'Connor in Warwick, New York, to toast the coming of spring. Jen always makes an effort to keep her time in the kitchen to a minimum during a party. For this luncheon, she planned a menu that could be prepared ahead of time and served at room temperature. This trick allows her to enjoy her gal pals for the brief time they are all together and keeps her guests feeling spoiled by not imposing on them to help prep or serve.

Five of the women—including the host—maintain gluten-free diets, and several of the women are vegetarians, so Jen has been sure to keep choices suitable for all. Marinated grilled meats take center stage and get kicked up a notch with local farmers market chutneys. A trio of colorful salads stand at the ready, and a gluten-free corn bread with honey butter rounds out the meal. A bean salad with a hint of Middle Eastern flavor and a slaw laden with cheese provide protein courses for those not eating meat.

Jen pulls together the serving pieces and place settings the night before. On the day of the luncheon, Kathy, a dear and helpful friend, comes over to help just after kids are taken to school. Jen cooks while Kathy pretties up the table with garden elements that give a nod to the coming of spring. Kathy opts to use burlap bags for place mats and sets out floral pottery and wee floral themed books as tokens of affection and party favors (Jen found the books on clearance and tucked them away for a special occasion). Kathy adds Jen's collection of miniature floral paintings by Earth Angels' artist Jennifer Lanne to the table for color and texture. Small gestures like these set a gentle and feminine mood.

As the gals arrive, pink "Moms' Day Out" punch is served in an odd assortment of sweet, vintage pressed-glass cups. Jen uses her punch bowl incessantly; it always sets a festive mood. At this luncheon it reminds the guests of the birthday parties they attended long ago when they were little girls.

Blue Cheese Slaw

Serves 8 to 12

Here's a twist on a classic cole slaw for those who love blue cheese. The red onion adds kick as well as color. The slaw is an unexpected and perfectly cool and creamy accompaniment to any grilled meat.

1 large head green cabbage, shredded, or 1 (14-oz.) bag preshredded cabbage (feel free to cheat!)

2 large carrots, shredded

1 medium red onion, sliced in rings, then in half (about 1 cup)

1½ cups crumbled blue cheese

1 cup good quality olive oil*

½ cup apple cider vinegar or balsamic vinegar (for a sharper flavor)*

Lots of fresh cracked pepper

Sea salt

*If you're in a hurry and need to cheat, substitute 1½ cups of your favorite bottled vinaigrette for the oil and vinegar.

1. Place cabbage, carrots, onion, blue cheese, vinegar, and olive oil in a large bowl. Sprinkle with pepper and sea salt. Toss until well combined. Cover and refrigerate for at least 4 hours.

2. Taste slaw and adjust seasonings; a touch more salt may be necessary depending on saltiness of blue cheese. Add more oil to moisten if needed.

"Contentment is a constant **feast**."

—Scottish proverb

Broccoli Bash

Serves 6

This recipe was given to Jen in 2005 by her hubby's cousin, Mark. It is an absolute favorite at their annual family reunion and 250 people can't be wrong! Most days, Jen follows Mark's recipe, but she's also adapted it using Craisins or currants instead of tomatoes, almonds instead of sunflower kernels, and so on, being creative with what she has in the pantry but maintaining the proportions.

- 12 bacon slices, cooked and crumbled
- 1 cup raw unsalted sunflower kernels
- ½ cup cherry tomatoes, sliced in half lengthwise
- 1 head of raw broccoli, cut into bite-size pieces
- 2 TB. red wine vinegar
- 1 cup mayonnaise (or substitute sour cream for a creamier version)

Combine all ingredients in a large bowl and mix well. Dish can be prepared and refrigerated up to 8 hours in advance. Serve at room temperature or slightly chilled.

At the dessert buffet, guests can prepare a treat just the way they like it: Hot fudge sundaes are a perfect self-serve solution! Further, a simple dessert standing at the ready makes it nicer if someone has to rush out early to fetch a kid or run an errand.

To assure that they will gather again, these gal pals set the date for their next lunch while they are still at the table. Someone offers to host and picks a date, even if it is months down the road. A round robin of e-mails a week or so before firms up the guest list. These ladies feel the more the merrier, and a changing roster of guests perpetuates the spirit of sharing. Those who attend leave the richer for having made the time to celebrate the simple joys of seeing old friends and meeting new ones.

Welcome Spring Fling

Fifi O'Neill

Fifi O'Neill's flair for beautiful details colors all she does. Years of restaurant ownership fed her passion for entertaining guests at intimate and memorable gatherings. In her charming cottage kitchen in Sarasota, Florida, this editor, writer, and stylist whips up delectable morsels and eye candy decorations with artistic ease. She gently inspires others to embrace their own inner host by living a delicious and elegant life.

123

Paris is without a doubt the pastry capital of the world, and it is here that Fifi O'Neill's journey began. As a child, she loved visiting the quintessential pastry shops the city is famous for, from the acclaimed Ladurée and Lenôtre to the more discreet but equally sublime shops tucked into every neighborhood. The artistic and tantalizing displays in the patisserie windows were like delicious, colorful paintings, and the scent of butter wafting down the street lured Fifi and her mother inside.

"These exceptional treats were crafted from ingredients at their seasonal peak. Their freshness, unadulterated flavor, and complementary toppings were as irresistible to the eye as they were to the taste buds," Fifi explains. "I found endless pleasure in their lightness, sweetness, and crunch."
(Continued on page 126.)

Thrills and Chills: Citrus Soufflés

Serves 6

To fill both lemons and limes, you will need to make two batches of filling—one using lemon juice and yellow food coloring and one using lime juice and green food coloring.

- 6 lemons or limes
- 1 cup white sugar
- 3 TB. cornstarch
- 1 envelope unflavored gelatin
- 1 cup water
- 1 lemon or lime, juiced
  Yellow or green food coloring
- 3 egg whites
- 1 cup heavy cream
  Waxed paper or foil
  Masking tape

For garnish:

  Lemon or lime wedges
  Citrus leaves
  Confectioners' sugar

1. Slice a little off the bottom of each lemon or lime to allow them to stand up. Slice off a small cap from each lemon or lime and set aside. Scoop out and discard the pulp.

2. In large saucepan, combine sugar, cornstarch, and gelatin. Add water and lemon or lime juice. Cook over medium heat, stirring until slightly thickened. Add a few drops of food coloring, one drop at a time, to create a pale yellow tint for the lemon soufflés or a pale green tint for the lime soufflés. Remove from heat and let cool. Chill until partially set, about 1 hour, stirring occasionally.

3. In small mixer bowl, beat egg whites until stiff but not dry. Fold into chilled mixture. Wash and dry bowl and chill it for 5 to 10 minutes. Add heavy cream to the chilled bowl and beat until stiff peaks form. Fold into chilled mixture.

4. Make 3-inch waxed paper or foil collars and tape in place at the top of each lemon or lime. Stand the fruit shells upright in a flat-bottomed dish. Pour chilled mixture into each fruit shell and up to the top of the collar. Place fruit in freezer for 6 hours or overnight or chill in refrigerator for 6 hours (for a softer texture). To serve, gently remove collar from fruit, top each soufflé with a reserved cap, and garnish with a lemon or lime wedge and citrus leaves as desired. Dust with confectioners' sugar.

Fifi credits her mother for her love of cooking. "Mom was an excellent cook and a pastry maven. Everything I know I owe to her. She was an amazing hostess, and one of her favorite ways to entertain was to hold after-theatre dessert parties." Years later, after Fifi married, she began to duplicate her parents' dessert parties for her own social gatherings. A feast of yummy desserts is perfect for a variety of celebrations, from birthdays to bridal and baby showers. As Fifi puts it, "What's not to love?"

Rose Pudding

Serves 6 to 8

2½ cups half-and-half or whole milk, divided
½ cup white sugar
Pinch of salt
3 TB. cornstarch
1 tsp. pure vanilla extract
1 tsp. rose water or rose syrup
1 TB. butter
Red food coloring

To coat rim:

Pink sugar crystals
Lemon juice
Rose petals (pesticide-free)

1. Heat 2 cups of the half-and-half or milk, sugar, and salt in a saucepan over medium heat until bubbles form at edges. Combine remaining ½ cup of half-and-half or milk and cornstarch in a bowl and stir until cornstarch is completely dissolved. Pour cornstarch mixture into the saucepan and continue to cook, stirring, for 5 minutes or until mixture thickens enough to coat the back of a metal spoon. Do not boil.

2. Remove mixture from heat and stir in vanilla, rose water or syrup, and butter. Add 2 drops of food coloring and mix well. Add additional food coloring if desired, one drop at a time, to reach desired shade of pink.

3. Pour some pink sugar crystals onto a plate. Moisten the rim of an 8-inch serving bowl with lemon juice and then press the rim into the sugar crystals to coat the rim. Pour the cooked pudding into the bowl. Chill for at least 2 hours. Before serving, sprinkle with sugar crystals and rose petals.

"**Food**: Part of the **spiritual** expression of the **French**, and I do not believe that they have ever **heard** of **calories**."

—Beverley Baxter

127

For an unforgettable day or night of indulgence, Fifi makes her desserts ahead of time and serves them buffet style. She creates a tiered bakeshop display by setting up serving pieces in various heights on a long table. Glasses of all shapes and sizes make individual servings of trifle, frozen soufflé, mousse, puddings, and parfaits extra delectable.

Food isn't the only component Fifi considers when planning a party. Little details, like lighting, table settings, and music also play into her selections. Giving the gathering a theme and setting the stage for the festivities is the magical part! When she hosted a Welcome Spring Fling outdoors, Fifi made a colorful maypole and hung seductive hammocks layered in soft floral linens from the trees. At the buffet, stacks of small

pastel-hued plates and napkins kept the spring mood flowing. Fifi invited her guests to bring a small token of the season to exchange with the other guests. The creative items people brought included a tiny nest, a potted herb, a floral napkin ring, and a birdhouse. "Once the guests arrive and see that they are, indeed, part of the celebration, then it is my turn to pamper them and make them feel very special," she says.

When the festivities wind down and her guests begin taking their leave, Fifi likes to send them home with cookies or flowers tucked inside her handmade paper cones. But most of all, she hopes every guest leaves inspired and ready to enjoy new ways to celebrate every day.

a FEAST for the EYES

Béatrice Peltre

"If it were easy, then everybody would be doing it." Those words of reinforcement were said to Béatrice Peltre by her husband, Philip, at times when she wasn't sure where she would fit in the food world. The Boston resident had no need to worry. Author, blogger, photographer, and food stylist, she found her place. She authored her first cookbook, *La Tartine Gourmande: Recipes for an Inspired Life*, her blog La Tartine Gourmande is internationally known, and she contributes to the *Boston Globe* food section. It may not be easy, but Béa has a flair for making it all look so easy, effortless, and elegant.

As a child in rural France, Béatrice Peltre grew up around fresh food. "My parents always had a vegetable garden," she says. "My father comes from a farming background." Eating and preparing fresh vegetables was a daily activity for her family of eaters. She loved baking, and her cultural roots instilled the European tradition of having a main meal at midday. "When I came here to the States, I thought it was strange that sandwiches were served for lunch instead of a hot meal," Béa recalls. "In France, lunch is a longer meal, usually hot, and prepared."

Béa's love for fresh food stayed with her even during her college years. "My roommate in college would come home and find our apartment filled with the scent of cooking garlic," Béa laughs. "I always prepared lunch before I left for the day, so it would be ready for me when I got home." Béa's mother, a schoolteacher with a strict schedule, instilled good eating habits by preparing meals ahead of time. "I always make sure I have groceries in the house and start thinking about what I want for dinner before I even start my day," says Béa. Although Béa moved to the States twelve years ago, her French culture continues to override any new American quick, takeout food habits.

"Whatever the season, I use what is in season for the freshest ingredients and for the color," says Béa. For this meal, Béa has chosen the bright colors of fall. Living in Boston, she takes advantage of the abundant farmers' markets and fresh seafood. Red kuri squash risotto is a meal that celebrates the fall season and is also a way to introduce vegetables to her adorable daughter, Lulu. "The colorful food is attractive. You have to want to eat food with the eye first," she says. "Lulu eats more risotto than we do! She can make quite a mess, but that is okay, I enjoy watching her," Béa laughs.
(Continued on page 134.)

Red Kuri Squash Risotto

Serves 4

- 1 small red kuri squash, seeded and cut into 1½-inch dice (1 lb. 2 oz. after preparation)*
- 3 TB. olive oil
  Sea salt and pepper
- 4 cups chicken stock
- 1 TB. butter
- 1 small red onion or shallot, diced
- 3 twigs of lemon thyme
- 1 cup Carnaroli rice or other risotto rice (like Arborio)
- ⅓ cup vermouth or dry white wine
- ½ cup finely grated pecorino or Parmesan
- 2 TB. crème fraîche
- 1 TB. chopped parsley

*Note: No need to peel the squash if it's organic

1. Preheat the oven to 375°F. Place the red kuri squash in a baking dish and drizzle with 2 TB. of the olive oil. Season with salt and pepper. Bake for 50 minutes or until the vegetable is tender. Transfer to the bowl of a food processor and purée finely; set aside.

2. In a saucepan, heat the chicken stock; keep warm on the side.

3. In a large pot, melt butter over medium heat. Add remaining 1 TB. olive oil, heat until warm, and add the onion and lemon thyme. Cook for 5 minutes, stirring, without browning and until the onion is soft.

4. Add the rice and stir to coat for 1 minute. Add the vermouth and cook until evaporated and absorbed by the rice. Add 1 cup of the chicken stock. Cook, stirring occasionally, adding more stock only when previous addition is absorbed. When you have only ½ cup of stock left, stir in the red kuri squash purée and the rest of the stock. Continue to cook just until the rice is al dente.

5. Remove from heat and stir in the pecorino, crème fraîche, and parsley. Discard the lemon thyme. Cover and let sit for 2 minutes. Serve immediately in individual bowls.

One is inclined to celebrate with Lulu and share her flavor-infused risotto with its finely chopped pecorino, diced squash with shallots, sea salt, and touches of vermouth and crème fraiche. That is, if Lulu would be willing to part with a portion!

After a belly full of warm risotto, Lulu is on the go. Béa asks her daughter, "*Tu veux allez te promener?*" (Do you want to go for a walk?) Celebrating a good meal doesn't just end with a wonderful dessert in the Peltre household but is extended with a nice walk. With a decidedly French flair for fashion, little Lulu grabs her petite purse and waits by the door for her mother. Although her food styling, photography, and writing are in demand, Béa is never happier than when she is celebrating with food and serving those she loves. "Food connects people to a place," she says. Béa is at her most content when she is in her own place, connected to her family—and serving them wonderful food, of course.

"One cannot **think** well, **love** well, **sleep** well, if one hasn't **eaten** well."

—Virginia Woolf

Bermuda TRIANGLE

A Percussion of Traditions to
Ring in the New Year

Beth Price

As a child, Beth Price had two reasons
not to like the first day of the year.
Coincidentally, her Bermudian husband
never liked the New Year holiday either.
Beth, who is the director of recipe
testing for David Leite's blog, Leite's
Culinaria, and assistant to cookbook
author and TV personality Nathalie
Dupree, decided to take back New Year's
Day for both of them by creating a new,
casual custom of their own.

"Christmas trees must be taken down on New Year's Day, or you will have bad luck the rest of the year. That was my family's tradition," says Beth Price about her childhood trees' early departures. "And that darned black-eyed pea. You have to eat one for good luck. I hated black-eyed peas," she recalls. Which explains why Beth hated the New Year growing up, but what about her husband, Clayton? "Clayton was born on December thirtieth, and his birthday always got lost in the shuffle of the holidays. It was usually tossed in on the first of the year," says Beth.

And so the story begins, sort of. Clayton is Bermudian, and in Bermuda, Christmas is celebrated for the twelve days beginning on Christmas day. The tree traditionally stays up until the end of the celebration, which concludes on January 5th with a black-tie party. Despite this deviation in their traditions, Beth and Clayton have common roots. "My ancestors shipwrecked in Bermuda in 1609, way before his ancestors arrived in 1642. Bermuda and the South actually have similar foods," Beth says knowledgably.

"Come **quick**! Have found **Heaven**!"

—Alfred Hutty, artist,
in a letter to his wife after stumbling upon
Charleston, South Carolina, in 1919

Bermuda Black Rum Banana Bread

Makes one 5 x 9-inch loaf

- 3 ripe bananas
- ½ cup vegetable oil
- ¼ cup milk
- ½ tsp. pure vanilla extract
- 1 tsp. Goslings Black Seal Rum
- 2 eggs
- 1¾ cups flour
- 1½ cups sugar
- 1 tsp. baking soda
- ½ tsp. salt
- ½ cup semisweet chocolate chips (add more chips for a real chocolate flavor)

For the glaze:

- 4 TB. butter
- 2 TB. water
- ½ cup white sugar
- ¼ cup rum

1. Preheat oven to 350°F. Grease a 5 x 9-inch loaf pan.

2. Using a potato masher, mash together the bananas, oil, milk, vanilla, rum, and eggs.

3. In a large bowl, combine the flour, sugar, baking soda, and salt. With a rubber spatula or wooden spoon, lightly fold the banana mixture into the dry ingredients. Add the chocolate chips and stir until combined and the batter is thick and chunky.

4. Pour the batter into the prepared pan and bake for 60 minutes or until the loaf is firm and begins to pull away from the sides. Remove from oven and let the bread cool in the pan. While cooling, prepare glaze.

5. For the glaze, melt butter in saucepan over medium heat. Stir in water and sugar and bring to a boil. Remove from heat and stir in rum. Drizzle glaze over bread.

Beth and Clayton have reclaimed the holiday by celebrating on the evening of New Year's Day. Friends can relax after a night of heavy partying, and Beth and Clayton don't feel the pressure of hosting a spectacular New Year's Eve party. "It is still a cocktail party," says Beth, "and the Charleston men love their bow ties, but it is casual."

Beth invites twenty or so couples, usually by word of mouth. "Some years I do handwritten invitations, and we hand-deliver them to keep things simple," she says. To enjoy the party, Beth chooses a menu she can prepare in advance. "Some years, we hire servers to walk around and serve guests to keep the flow of the party going," Beth says. This year, she created a menu that combines Southern and Bermudian flavors in the New Year's tradition.

Beth uses family heirlooms to elegantly decorate the buffet table. Flowers are placed in silver mint julep cups that were engraved and given to their children at their christenings. She serves Hoppin' John Hummus as a way to "get that good luck in and disguise the black-eyed pea." Beth also prepares biscuits and collard green soup, which she serves in her husband's grandmother's demitasse cups. And no Bermudian event would be complete without at least one recipe containing black rum! Beth bakes a Bermuda black rum banana bread so shipwreck-worthy, even her ancestors would do it all over again. She chooses these recipes not only for their cultural influences, but also because she can prepare them several days in advance so as not to stress about food the day of the party.

Hoppin' John Hummus

For party favors, Beth gives bottles of Lamboll Street Loquat Liqueur, which she must store in a cool place for six months before it is ready. "When I first moved here, I was amazed at all the loquat trees," says Beth. "I would send my children out to collect the loquats and began making the liqueur, a true Bermudian flavor." Beth also gives Bermuda Sherry Pepper Sauce at the New Year. These "bird peppers" are steeped in dry cooking sherry and then stored in pretty glass jars. The spicy peppers flavor the sherry, which is used in Bermuda fish chowder, stews, and soups.

So exactly how does this recipe tester, cook, assistant to cookbook authors, and foodie celebrate her husband's birthday? By taking him out to dinner, of course, on his real birthday. "We celebrate the way he wants to, with family."

142

Collard Greens Soup

Makes 4 to 6 entrées or 24 demitasse servings

   2 lb. collard greens
   ¼ lb. bacon
   1 cup diced onion
   ½ cup diced celery
   1 tsp. black pepper
   8 oz. country ham or other smoky ham
   1 quart chicken stock
   3 Yukon Gold potatoes, peeled and diced
   1 cup heavy cream
   1 TB. olive oil
      Salt and pepper

1. Fill a basin with cool water, submerge the collard greens, and gently agitate to remove any loose dirt. Rinse the greens and dry on paper towels. Cut away the center vein of each leaf and discard. Roughly chop the leaves.

2. In a large heavy pot over medium-high heat, cook the bacon until all the fat is rendered. Remove the bacon and reserve for another use.

3. Add the onion, celery, pepper, ham, and collards to the bacon drippings and cook over low heat until onions are translucent. Add the chicken stock and simmer for 45 minutes. Remove ham from pot and set aside.

4. Place potatoes in a separate pot, add water to cover, and simmer until tender, about 15 minutes. Add cream and cooked potatoes to the collards and stir to combine. Working in batches, process the soup in a food processor until smooth. Strain though a chinois or fine sieve into a large bowl, pressing the solids against the side to remove all the liquid. Reserve the solids and set aside. Adjust the seasonings in the purée, adding salt and pepper to taste. (Consistency of soup can be adjusted by addition of cream, broth, or potatoes.)

5. Trim the reserved ham of all fat and discard. Cut ham into a ¼-inch dice. Heat the olive oil in a sauté pan until the oil begins to shimmer. Sauté the ham until lightly browned, about 2 minutes. Set aside on a paper towel to drain.

6. To serve, ladle soup into serving bowls or cups and top with a bit of the reserved collard solids and sautéed ham. To make the soup even "luckier," add a few cooked black-eyed peas on top. Pass Bermuda Sherry Pepper Sauce on the side.

Bermuda Sherry Pepper Sauce

   1 (16-oz.) bottle sherry cooking wine
   ¼ cup bird peppers or other small red peppers

Combine peppers and sherry in a clean sterilized jar and let sit for several weeks. To speed up the process, the peppers can be lightly simmered in enough vinegar to cover, drained, and added to the sherry.

My SISTER'S Wedding

Jael Rattigan
FRENCH BROAD CHOCOLATES

Jael Rattigan found her place in the world, creating artisanal chocolates and handmade desserts in the lovely mountain town of Asheville, North Carolina. At her downtown dessert restaurant, French Broad Chocolate Lounge, and through her website, this passionate foodie and locavore provides her chocolate-loving community with decadent, small luxuries.

In the spacious kitchen on the third floor of her restaurant, French Broad Chocolate Lounge, Jael Rattigan crafts her dark chocolate turtles: housemade salted honey caramel and heirloom pecans, hand-dipped in organic dark chocolate. The kitchen, painted in her signature light blue and chocolate brown, fills with natural light and the aroma of freshly baked sweets. "It has the warmth and feel of a home kitchen, but with more professional toys," grins Jael. These edible works of art were packaged in small boxes tied with red ribbon, and given to guests as the favors at her sister Kellie's wedding in rural Minnesota.

The intimate outdoor ceremony took place at their mom's lakeside apple orchard. All of the details were inspired by the orchard's natural beauty. Mason jars filled with tiny green apples, gingham accents, and local antique green hydrangeas set the tone for a casually elegant event. Kellie and her dad arrived in a picturesque horse-drawn carriage. Simple picnic food was served family-style, and guests dined under the canopy of apple trees in the orchard.

The wedding cake was Jael's gift to the bride and groom. She created a four-tiered vanilla cake with raspberry buttercream filling, and vanilla bean buttercream icing. The decorations were simple and romantic: hand-piped dots of buttercream, antique gold ribbon, and a crown of fresh red roses. The flour, butter and eggs were Minnesota grown, and the local raspberries were grown by the Hutterite community down the road. Jael used a cake recipe from the *Joy of Cooking*, which she then presented to Kellie and Jim. The handwritten inscription in the front cover read:

Dear **Kellie & Jim**,

In our family, **cooking** is how we celebrate, feeding people is

how we show our **love**. It's our favorite thing to do together. May you love each other and cook together for a long **time**.

love, Jael

Recipe

Kellie and Jim's Wedding Cake

Makes one three-layer 9-inch cake

Adapted from *Joy of Cooking*

For a four-tiered wedding cake, use 6-, 8-, 10-, and 12-inch cake pans, triple the White Cake recipe, and triple the Raspberry Buttercream recipe.

Part 1: White Cake

14	ozs. (3½ cups) pastry flour
1	TB. + 1 tsp. baking powder
½	tsp. salt
8	oz. (1 cup) milk, at room temperature
1	tsp. pure vanilla extract
8	oz. (1 cup) butter, at room temperature
12.5	oz. (1⅔ cup) sugar
11	oz. egg whites (from 8 large eggs), at room temperature
⅜	tsp. cream of tartar
2.5	oz. (⅓ cup) sugar

1. Preheat oven to 350°F. Line the bottoms of three 9-inch cake pans with parchment paper.

2. Whisk together flour, baking powder, and salt and then sift twice. In a separate bowl, combine milk and vanilla.

3. Cream butter in a stand mixer for 30 seconds. Gradually add sugar to butter and beat on high, 3 to 5 minutes, until lightened in color and texture. With mixer on low speed, add the flour in three parts, alternating with the milk in two parts.

4. In a separate mixing bowl of the stand mixer, beat the egg whites and cream of tartar on medium speed until soft peaks form. Gradually add the sugar and beat on high until peaks are stiff but not dry.

5. Fold one-quarter of the egg whites into the batter, then fold in the remaining whites. Scrape batter into prepared pans and bake until springy and set, and a toothpick in the center comes out clean, 25 to 30 minutes. Cool in pans on a cooling rack.

Tip: For accuracy in baking, Jael always weighs ingredients (except small amounts like salt and baking powder). Her recipes include volumetric measures for those who don't have a scale.

144

It seemed like only yesterday that Jael was planning another family wedding for her brother, Shae. At the reception, she flirted with a cute bartender named Dan, and by the end of the evening, the pair had exchanged phone numbers. Seven years, two kids, and two restaurants later, they continue to collaborate and grow. "Dan is the visionary. I imagine him to be a helium balloon, and I'm the tether," Jael says. "He leads me to ideas I couldn't have imagined, and together, we manifest our dreams into reality."

In 2004, the couple dropped out of graduate school, drove to Costa Rica in a vegetable oil–powered, 40-foot-long school bus-turned-RV, and opened Bread & Chocolate, a café and dessert shop, to rave reviews. "It was a very empowering experience," says Jael. Two years later, they sold the café to one of their chefs (who operates it to this day) and drove the same school bus back to the States.

Settling in Asheville, Dan and Jael created French Broad Chocolates, a line of artisanal chocolate truffles sold at local farmers markets and on their website. A year later, with big ideas and a small budget, they converted a 19th century brick building into French Broad Chocolate Lounge. Their unique gathering place filled a niche in Asheville, and soon the line of tourists and locals alike snaked out the door. French Broad Chocolates just celebrated four years in business, and their customers are still smitten. With every bite, Jael's chocolates give us all something to celebrate.

Recipe

Part 2: Swiss Vanilla Bean Buttercream

- 8 oz. egg whites (from 6 eggs)
- 1 lb. sugar (2 cups)
- 2 vanilla beans, split and seeds scraped
- 1 lb. 4 oz. butter (2½ cups)

1. Put the egg whites and sugar in the bowl of a stand mixer and whisk together until the sugar is blended into the egg whites.

2. Place the bowl over a saucepan of simmering water and whisk gently and constantly until the sugar dissolves and the mixture reaches 160°F.

3. Immediately transfer the bowl to the mixer and beat on high speed until the meringue is thick and glossy and holds stiff peaks.

4. With mixer on medium, gradually add butter and mix until buttercream is light and creamy.

5. Split the vanilla bean pods in two with a knife and scrape out the seeds.

6. Add the seeds to the buttercream and mix to combine.

7. Set aside 14 oz. buttercream (about 2 cups) to make raspberry buttercream.

Part 3: Raspberry Purée

- 24 oz. frozen raspberries
- 4 oz. (½ cup) sugar
- 2 tsp. lemon juice

1. Thaw frozen raspberries and force the juice through a strainer. Run the pulp through a food mill to remove seeds. Set puree aside.

2. Pour the juice into a small saucepan. Boil over medium heat until juice reduces to one third of its original volume. Add the sugar and lemon juice to the reduction and cook until sugar is dissolved. Remove from heat. Add the puree and stir to combine. Cool in refrigerator.

Recipe

Part 4: Raspberry Buttercream

14 oz. (2 cups) Swiss vanilla bean buttercream

3 oz. (⅓ cup) raspberry puree

1. Place softened Swiss Vanilla Bean Buttercream in the bowl of stand mixer.

2. Add puree all at once and beat to combine, scraping bowl as necessary

Part 5: Cake Assembly

1. Release the sides of the cake from the pan with a small knife blade and invert onto a cardboard cake circle (cake will be upside-down).

2. Spoon 1 cup Raspberry Buttercream onto the cake and spread in an even layer.

3. Invert the next cake layer on top and spread with 1 cup Raspberry Buttercream.

4. Invert the third and final cake layer on top.

5. Cover the entire cake with a thin layer of Swiss Vanilla Bean Buttercream; this layer, called the crumb coat, serves as a "spackle" coat under the outer layer of icing. Refrigerate until cool.

6. Cover surface and sides with Swiss Vanilla Bean Buttercream. Smooth with an offset icing spatula. If desired, pipe dots of buttercream on the surface, using a small plain tip.

7. Any remaining buttercream can be used to pipe a border on the top, or refrigerated for another use for up to two weeks.

Note: A cake turntable and an offset icing spatula make assembly much easier.

"Tell **me** what you **eat**, and I will tell **you who** you are."

—Jean Anthelme Brillat-Savarin

147

chapsgirl + farmchick = friendship

A celebration of friendship at Chaps

Celeste Shaw

Celeste Shaw, born and raised a Montana girl, loved cooking and serving from an early age. Her grandmother, Selma, was a homesteader who rarely missed an opportunity to celebrate life's precious moments. "Although my grandmother was a wonderful cook, I think what she served best was her sweet self," says Celeste. Selma's legacy continues on at Chaps and Cake, Celeste's shop in Spokane, Washington, and the site of the 2010 Farm Chicks vendor gathering, where women arrived as acquaintances and left as friends.

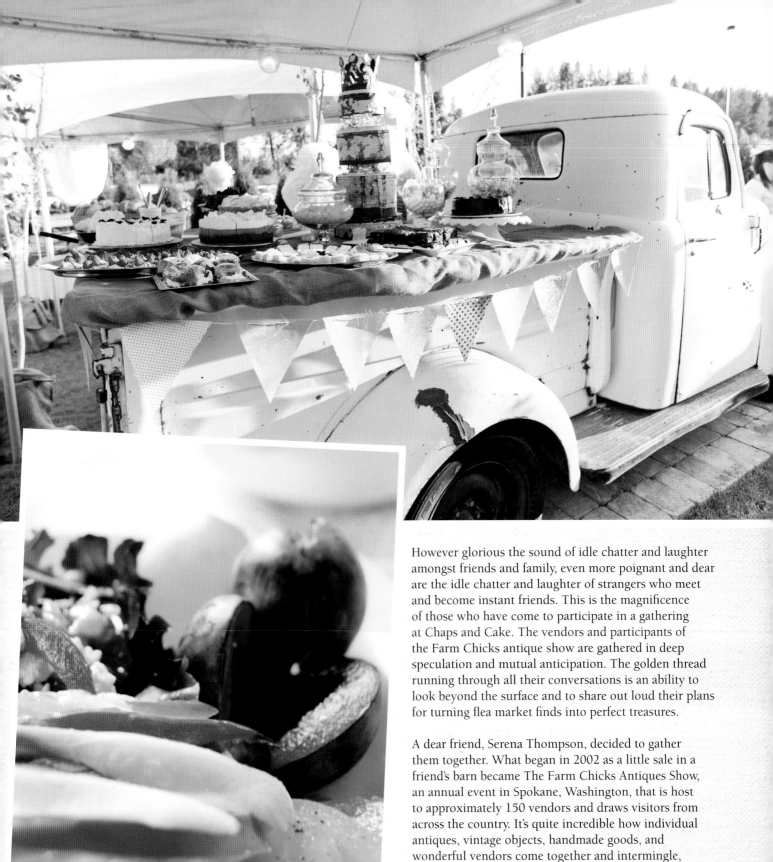

However glorious the sound of idle chatter and laughter amongst friends and family, even more poignant and dear are the idle chatter and laughter of strangers who meet and become instant friends. This is the magnificence of those who have come to participate in a gathering at Chaps and Cake. The vendors and participants of the Farm Chicks antique show are gathered in deep speculation and mutual anticipation. The golden thread running through all their conversations is an ability to look beyond the surface and to share out loud their plans for turning flea market finds into perfect treasures.

A dear friend, Serena Thompson, decided to gather them together. What began in 2002 as a little sale in a friend's barn became The Farm Chicks Antiques Show, an annual event in Spokane, Washington, that is host to approximately 150 vendors and draws visitors from across the country. It's quite incredible how individual antiques, vintage objects, handmade goods, and wonderful vendors come together and intermingle, and it's all the more special at Chaps and Cake.

Every celebration is a memoir, a testament to the power of joy. In Europe, when people go on vacation or away for the weekend, they call it a holiday. The idea of celebration—a holiday—creates a sparkle of connection throughout life. People celebrate birth, love, accomplishment, change, friendship, ownership, togetherness, separation—the list of reasons for celebrating is infinite. Every celebration is an invitation to the ultimate dance, to engage and awaken the original cadence of mind and soul. The honor of your presence is very much requested. Won't you join in recollecting a few precious sparkles? At Chaps and Cake, no RSVP is required.

Barn House Martini

Makes 1 cocktail

Red food coloring

Raw sugar

Lemon juice or water

1 oz. XXX mango passion liqueur

2 oz. grapefruit vodka

1 scoop lemon sorbet

1. Stir a few drops of red food coloring into the raw sugar to tint it pink. Dip the rim of a martini glass into lemon juice or water and then into the pink sugar to coat the rim.

2. Add the mango passion liqueur and vodka to a martini shaker and shake well.

3. Place the lemon sorbet in the martini glass. Pour the cocktail into the glass and serve.

"Be **kind** always."
—Mother Teresa

151

At this Farm Chicks celebration at Chaps and Cake, people once again see with childlike eyes the beauty of handcrafted decorations and paper flowers, glitter and candles. They taste showoff creations that encompass the diversity of generations and the flavors of ethnic origins. The smells of celebrations are like going to the fair, where the air clutches the scents of pleasure and cuisine. At dressup celebrations, the smell of perfume is intoxicating. Like landing in an international airport, so excited to be shopping duty-free, it's as if every friend who wears great perfume is happily waiting to greet you.

Laughing, singsong talking, music, the sounds of cooking! *Shhh*, just listen and hear it. Exclaiming with overwhelming delight, the people hug, kiss, and embrace every detail. There's eating food with fingers, that Montana farmgirl peculiarity. Touches of indulgence and luxury and all things "new" combine with the old, the chippy, and the tattered. By combining past and present, this event inspires what yet will be.

There are certainly no rules when it comes to creating a moment of celebration. Moments of grandeur, moments of intimacy—both are golden, imaginative, illuminating and draw motivation and confidence from one another. More important than the food, the presents, and the speeches, it is the sweet amazing grace and charm of each and every participant that is the true cause for celebration. The party is almost over, the dinner was delicious, and now it's time for one more thing … dessert, from Cake, of course.

Lemon Bars

Makes 25 bars

- 3 cups all-purpose flour
- 1 cup confectioners' sugar, plus more for topping
- ¼ tsp. salt
- 1½ cups (3 sticks) unsalted butter, cold, cut into pieces

For the lemon filling:

- 8 large eggs
- 4 cups granulated sugar
- ⅔ cup all-purpose flour
- 1½ cups freshly squeezed lemon juice
- 1 TB. lemon zest

1. Preheat oven to 350°F. In a large bowl, whisk together 3 cups flour, confectioners' sugar, and salt. Using a pastry blender, cut in the butter until the largest pieces are the size of peas. Press mixture into the bottom of an ungreased 10 x 15-inch rimmed baking pan. Bake 20 to 30 minutes, until golden. Cool.

2. In a medium bowl, whisk together the eggs, sugar, and ⅔ cup flour until combined. Whisk in the lemon juice and zest until combined. Pour filling onto crust.

3. Return pan to oven and bake for 30 minutes, rotating pan halfway through, until set. Cool completely. Dust with powdered sugar and cut into bars approximately 2 x 3 inches. Bars can be stored in an airtight container in the refrigerator for up to one week.

A FARM CHICK AT HOME

Serena Thompson

Serena Thompson is founder of the Farm Chicks antiques show, co-author with Teri Edwards of *Farm Chicks in the Kitchen*, and the author of *A Farm Chicks Christmas*. But what this blogger, author, and antiques show promoter loves most is putting together spur-of-the-moment celebrations for her own family at their country home outside of Spokane, Washington.

Being the mom of four boys, Serena Thompson has found that any occasion can be made special with just a little extra attention. When she was a girl, Serena loved visiting San Francisco's Chinatown where she purchased paper lanterns, cocktail umbrellas, and colorful origami paper. Whenever she wanted to make things feel festive, she'd go to her special Chinatown stock of goodies, string up a few lights, fold up paper frogs, and add paper umbrellas to water glasses. Just a few simple additions made everyday family occurrences feel a little more special. Soon she began looking for any excuse to stage a celebration. Her sister made the honor roll? Celebrate! Her dad took a new job? Celebrate! The wild strawberries are blooming? Celebrate!

Lunchbox Creams

Makes 1 dozen

- ¾ cup granulated sugar
- ½ cup butter
- 2 TB. water
- 1 cup semisweet chocolate chips
- 1 tsp. pure vanilla extract
- 2 eggs
- 2 cups flour
- ¼ tsp. baking soda

For the filling:

- ¼ cup butter, at room temperature
- ¼ cup vegetable shortening
- 1 cup confectioners' sugar
- 1 tsp. pure vanilla extract

1. Preheat oven to 350°F. Lightly butter a baking sheet.

2. Combine sugar, butter, and water in a mixing bowl and microwave until butter is melted. Add chocolate chips and vanilla; whisk until smooth. Cool mixture for about 5 minutes.

3. Add eggs one at a time, whisking well after each addition. Whisk in flour and baking soda until completely combined.

4. Scoop dough out onto the buttered baking sheet, using either a 2-TB. scoop or by the heaping TB. Leave at least 1 inch of space between each scoop of dough. Bake for approximately 8 minutes or until the cookies feel slightly firm when touched in the center and finger leaves a small indentation. Remove from baking sheet and cool on a wire rack. While cookies are cooling, prepare the filling.

5. For the filling, combine butter, shortening, confectioners' sugar, and vanilla in a mixing bowl. Beat until light and fluffy. Spread filling on the bottom of half of the cookies. Add remaining cookies on top, sandwiching the filling in between.

And as she grew older, Serena realized that simple acts like baking a plate of cookies for a neighbor or a pie for a teacher were special too. Although such treats weren't the same as full-blown parties, they did celebrate people in Serena's life and gave her a way to connect with them through something special she had created just for them. Thus her love of baking and celebrating was born.

Birthdays, anniversaries, and holidays are always a big deal in Serena's house, but so are other milestones. She discovered that celebrating a transition like returning to school really makes a difference in how her children react to it.

"My **play** was a complete **success**. The audience was a **failure**."

—Oscar Wilde

Big and Chewy Peanut Butter Cookies

Makes 20 large cookies

- 1 cup (2 sticks) unsalted butter, at room temperature
- 1 cup packed brown sugar
- 1 cup crunchy peanut butter
- ½ cup honey
- 2 tsp. pure vanilla extract
- 2 large eggs
- 2 cups all-purpose flour
- 1 cup whole wheat flour
- 1 tsp. baking soda
- ¼ tsp. salt
- 1 cup salted peanuts, for topping (optional)
- 2 cups chocolate chunks or chips (optional)

1. Preheat the oven to 375°F.

2. Cream the butter in a large bowl with an electric mixer on medium speed. Beat in the brown sugar, peanut butter, honey, vanilla, and eggs, mixing until well combined.

3. Stir in the all-purpose and whole wheat flours, baking soda, and salt with a wooden spoon until completely incorporated. Stir in chocolate chunks (optional).

4. Drop the dough by ¼ cup onto baking sheets, spaced about 3 inches apart. If you like, press at least four peanuts into the top of each cookie or press a crosshatch pattern with the tines of a fork. Bake until lightly browned, 12 to 15 minutes. Transfer the cookies to a wire rack to cool. The cookies will appear slightly undercooked in the center but will firm up as they cool. Store in an airtight container.

School lets out in June for the Thompson boys, and they couldn't be more excited. Summer break in the Pacific Northwest is a boy's wonderland, and each moment is thoroughly enjoyed. Special backpacking trips with Dad, brother sleep-outs in the fort, campouts at the lake, movies on the deck, rafting on the Salmon River, hiking, biking, and swimming in ice-cold mountain streams. Naturally, when September rolls around, the thought of school holds little appeal. Serena and her husband, Colin, felt it was important to present the new school year as a positive thing in their boys' lives.

The solution? A back-to-school party, of course!

This year, Serena decided to throw a cookie party, complete with the cookies her boys love best and colorful decorations all around. Toy trucks work as perfect centerpieces, her favorite vintage Richard Scarry books make darling placemats, and old individual glass milk bottles prove to be the vessels of choice for ice-cold milk.

This simple celebration was made special with homemade treats and familiar objects found around her home. For Serena and her family, any day can be a party. It's all in how you look at it.

159

Feeding HER SOUL

Discovering the Ingredients of a Meaningful Life

Molly Wizenberg

A Seattle transplant, Molly Wizenberg authored her first cookbook, *A Homemade Life*, while writing her award-winning food blog, Orangette. She pens a monthly column for *Bon Appétit*, and she also produces a podcast called Spilled Milk with fellow food-writer Matthew Amster-Burton. Molly loves to create new recipes for her own kitchen and for Delancey, the New York-inspired restaurant she owns with her husband.

"I worked hard in school, and I always thought I would be a scientist," says Molly Wizenberg. As a little girl, Molly spent time in the kitchen creating "mixtures." Her mother allowed her to use any and as many ingredients as she wanted. "Mixing it up" became the connecting thread in Molly's life as a globetrotter, student, blogger, freelance writer, columnist, podcaster, photographer, cook, author of a *New York Times* best seller, and restaurateur. (Continued on page 164.)

Pan-fried Chiles with Lemon, Garlic and Sea Salt

Serves 2 or 3

¼ cup vegetable oil

8 oz. fresh Padron or shishito chiles, left whole with stems and seeds intact

¼ tsp. table salt

2 large cloves garlic, thinly sliced

¾ tsp. lemon juice, or to taste

Coarse sea salt, to taste

1. Warm a 12-inch skillet over high heat. When the pan is hot, add the oil, swirling to coat. As soon as the oil shimmers—it won't take long—add the peppers and table salt. They should crackle wildly. Stir constantly over the heat, shaking the pan. The chiles will begin to blister after only a minute or so.

2. After cooking about 2 minutes, when the chiles are blistered over about half of their surface area, add the garlic. Continue to stir constantly until the chiles are blistered all over, about 4 minutes. Depending on their size, some will be al dente and some will be softer; this is fine.

3. Transfer the chiles to a plate lined with a paper towel and drain briefly. Toss with lemon juice, season generously with coarse sea salt, and serve immediately.

Pickled Peppers with Shallots and Thyme

Makes 1 quart

This recipe will work for almost any kind of sweet or mild pepper. I don't recommend full-sized bell peppers because the flesh isn't as dense and crunchy as the flesh of smaller peppers, which are more flavorful.

- 1 lb. small sweet or mild peppers, sliced crosswise into ¼-inch-thick rounds, seeded
- 2 medium shallots, thinly sliced, separated into rings
- 2 cups white wine vinegar
- 3 TB. water
- ½ cup sugar
- 5 sprigs fresh thyme
- 2 large cloves garlic, thinly sliced
- ¼ tsp. red pepper flakes, or to taste
- Generous pinch of kosher salt

1. Put the peppers and shallots in a medium bowl.

2. In a medium saucepan, combine the vinegar, water, sugar, thyme, garlic, red pepper flakes, and salt. Place over medium heat and slowly bring to a boil. As soon as the mixture boils, remove the pan from the heat and pour the hot brine over the peppers and shallots. Cover the bowl with a lid and set aside at room temperature for 5 minutes, allowing the peppers to steam and soften slightly.

3. Remove the lid and let the mixture cool completely to room temperature. Transfer to a quart-size jar and refrigerate at least 4 hours before serving. Peppers taste best after a day or more of brining. Serve them on pizza or on an antipasto plate with cured meats. They're also delicious with sharp white cheddar and crusty bread or in a grilled cheese sandwich.

"I never really had a plan," says Molly. "I was a good student and did well in a lot of subjects. I loved writing." In their Oklahoma City home, her father created the savory dishes, while her mother did most of the baking. With joie de vivre in the kitchen, surrounded by great food and a family of eaters, Molly naturally became a good student of life as well. She went on to college and graduate school, but when she traveled to Paris for work related to her PhD anthropology program, she found her old loves of writing and food reawakened. "Here I was with this journal to write down my research, but instead, I was filling the pages with notes on all of the bakeries and cheese shops and what I was cooking!" she laughs.

"We are involved in a **life** that passes **understanding** and our **highest** business is our daily life."

—John Cage

Molly quit the research program and started a blog to gain experience and find a voice as a food writer. Posting her first entry of Orangette in July 2004, Molly was among the first surge of food bloggers. Over time, it became her love connection to her future husband and business partner.

Brandon, a food lover living in New York City, began reading Orangette. He wrote Molly an email and she responded. After several weeks of e-mail correspondence, they exchanged phone numbers, and eventually Brandon flew out to Seattle to meet this beautiful blogger in person. One could say it was love at first "byte." Brandon moved to Seattle and married Molly. But he missed his New York City pizza. Brandon had worked in restaurants since he was 15 years old, so together he and Molly opened Delancey, a restaurant that allows Brandon to happily knead Seattle's most highly acclaimed wood oven–fired pizzas.

With toppings like housemade pork fennel sausage, Padron chiles, crimini mushrooms, and La Quercia prosciutto, it is no surprise that Delancey's customers are willing to wait up to two hours for a taste. Molly creates the starters on the menu with delectable ingredients such as local arugula, preserved Meyer lemons, sheep's milk feta, and marinated olives. She also works with pastry chef Brandi Henderson to concoct a rotating menu of mouthwatering desserts, such as raspberry pavlova and lemon pound cake.

Delancey is a welcoming neighborhood place. "The open kitchen lets us see people's faces when they eat our pizza," says Molly. Whether she is standing at her own kitchen counter or behind the pizza counter at Delancey's, Molly loves being part of this community of food and people. The anthropologist in Molly puts it this way: "Food is an incredible way to try to see where it is we come from, who we are, and who we want to be. I find that fascinating."

Green Goddess Dressing

This dressing is delicious on almost any type of salad greens. At Delancey, we serve it on Bibb lettuce with small pieces of crunchy bacon, chopped oven-roasted tomatoes, and slivers of fresh herbs. The dressing is also very good on a salad of romaine, cucumber, beets, and avocado. You can also use it as a dip for crudités.

Makes 2 cups

- 1 small shallot, finely chopped
- 1 clove garlic, finely chopped
- 3 TB. white wine vinegar
- 1 tsp. lemon juice
- ½ tsp. lime juice
- 1 oil-packed anchovy, rinsed and very finely chopped
- ½ ripe medium avocado
- ¾ cup olive oil
- ½ cup cream
- 3 TB. chopped Italian parsley
- 1 TB. chopped tarragon
- 2 TB. chopped cilantro
- 2 TB. chopped basil
- ¼ tsp. salt, plus more to taste
  Pinch of sugar

1. In a medium bowl, combine the shallot, garlic, vinegar, lemon juice, and lime juice. Set aside for 10 minutes.

2. Add the anchovy and avocado and mash well with a fork. Gradually whisk in the olive oil and cream, as though you were making a thin mayonnaise. Add the herbs, salt, and sugar and whisk to combine. Taste dressing and adjust the seasoning as needed.

A Jewelry PARTY

Dana Wootton

What happens when a food blogger/ caterer throws a party for a local jeweler? Food, fun, and shopping! Step inside Dana's kitchen in Seattle, Washington, for a sneak peek at some of the party food favorites she loves to share with friends and family.

Of the many types of parties she hosts, Dana likes the chance to celebrate a person the best. Whether it is a birthday party, a baby shower, or highlighting the work of a talented artist, she loves to gather people around to celebrate. When the opportunity came up to host a jewelry party for a local artist, she jumped at the chance. The fact that it was close to the holiday gift-giving season made it all the sweeter.

Dana has a history of hosting jewelry parties. For years she did a party every holiday season for a friend. She would invite all her nearest and dearest and would make food for everyone to enjoy while shopping for gifts, or for themselves. It gave her a chance to test out new recipes for appetizers and treats. Once that friend moved away, the jewelry parties stopped. But now, with a new artist friend to spotlight, it looks like the jewelry parties may start up again!

Dana also creates beautiful things—it just so happens that her beautiful things are of the food variety. She has worked as a personal chef and catered small parties around her hometown of Seattle, but her favorite creative venue is in her own home, surrounded by friends and family. Between hosting at least three dinner parties a month along with Thanksgiving dinner, Christmas Eve dinner, and various birthdays throughout the year, she gets the chance to practice a lot of recipes.

As someone who has loved to cook all her adult life, Dana Wootton always dreamed of having a big kitchen. She has thrown countless parties—everything from intimate gatherings of a few friends to large blowout summer parties with upwards of 100 people. She and her husband knew that no matter how many places there are to gather, no matter how lovely the weather outside, everyone always ends up in the kitchen. When they found a house with not only a large cooking space but with an open floor plan that could include everyone, they jumped at the chance to make it home.

Cheeseball with Cumin, Mint and Pistachios

Makes 12 to 16 appetizer servings

Adapted from *The New York Times Cookbook*

Recipe for cheeseball was adapted from *The Essential New York Times Cookbook: Classic Recipes for a New Century* by Amanda Hesser (William Morrow Cookbooks, 1990)

- 1 cup (8 ozs.) cream cheese, at room temperature
- ½ cup (4 ozs.) goat cheese (chévre), at room temperature
- 1 TB. lemon juice
- Grated zest of 1 lemon
- ½ cup grated Pecorino Romano, preferably Fulvi
- 1 tsp. toasted and ground coriander seeds
- 1 tsp. toasted and ground cumin seeds
- ½ cup finely sliced celery hearts, with leaves
- ⅓ cup chopped mint
- ¼ tsp. freshly ground black pepper
- Sea salt
- ⅓ cup salted pistachios, coarsely ground

1. In a large bowl, beat cream cheese and goat cheese with a wooden spoon until creamy and light. Beat in lemon juice and lemon zest. Fold in Pecorino Romano, coriander, cumin, celery, mint, and pepper. Season to taste with sea salt.

2. Lay a large piece of plastic wrap on counter. Using a spatula, scrape cheese mixture onto center of plastic. Pull up sides of plastic wrap and form cheese into a ball. Wrap tightly, place in a bowl and chill in refrigerator for at least 2 hours.

3. Pour ground pistachios into a shallow bowl. Unwrap cheeseball and roll it in nuts until coated. Lay ball on a serving plate, cover with plastic wrap, and chill until ready to serve. A half hour before serving, unwrap cheeseball and let it come to room temperature. Serve with very thin plain crackers.

Curried Tofu-and-Avocado Dip

Makes about 2 cups

 1   (12-oz.) box silken tofu
 2   large Hass avocados, peeled, pitted, and coarsely chopped
 ⅔   cup low-fat plain yogurt
     Zest and juice of 1 lime
 1   garlic clove
 2   tsp. honey
 1½ tsp. curry powder
 ¼   cup chopped mint
 2   TB. chopped cilantro
     Olive oil
     Salt and freshly ground pepper

1. In a food processor, combine everything except the olive
   oil and salt and pepper. Process until completely smooth,
   adding olive oil if too thick.

2. When dip is smooth and at the desired consistency, season
   to taste with salt and pepper. Chill until cold. Serve with
   pita chips and fresh vegetables for dipping.

Note: This dip will keep for two days in the refrigerator, but the
top layer will turn brownish because of the avocado. I suggest
storing it in a cylinder-shaped container (such as a large
yogurt container) because it has a smaller top surface area.

For this party, the jewelry artist set up her wares
in the space between the kitchen and the living
room. It was an open house from 6:00 to 9:00 PM,
which gave everyone plenty of time to browse,
chat, munch on goodies, and sip champagne.
Dana made sure she had enough food for people
to nibble on and enough variety to allow people
to eat dinner if they wanted. For this party, she
made some well-loved recipes from her vast
repertoire of favorites, all classics with a twist.

The party was a big success with lots of gifts
bought and most of the food gone. Dana is
already looking forward to next year.

"Walk **tall**, or baby,
don't **walk** at all."

—Bruce Springsteen

r.s.v.p.

Wendy Addison
Marcia Ceppos
(page 8)
www.Wendyaddison.blogspot.com
www.wendyaddisonstudio.com
www.tinseltrading.com

Susan Branch
(page 14)
www.susanbranch.com

Orianne Cosentino
(page 20)
www.upchefcreek.com

Sandy Coughlin
(page 26)
www.reluctantentertainer.com
reluctantentertainer@yahoo.com

Cheryl Day
(page 32)
www.backinthedaybakery.com

Marina Drasnin
(page 38)
www.marinaartiste.com
Drasninmarina@aol.com

Ree Drummond
(page 42)
www.ThePioneerWoman.com

Angie Dudley
(page 50)
www.bakerella.com

Helene Dujardin
(page 84)
www.tarteletteblog.com
www.helenedujardin.com

Ashley English
(page 56)
www.small-measure.blogspot.com
www.designspongeonline.com/
category/small-measures
ashleyadamsenglish@gmail.com

Shea Fragoso
Debbie Murray
(page 110)
www.AGildedLife.com
www.whathappensnext.typepad.com

Christine Hoffman
(page 64)
www.piesandaprons.blogspot.com
christinechoffman@gmail.com

Patricia Mackey
(page 72)
www.tippystockton.com
www.tippystocktonblog.blogspot.com
tippystockton@aol.com

Tricia Martin
(page 78)
www.eatingisart.com
tricia@eatingisart.com

Andrea Meyers
(page 90)
www.andreasrecipes.com

Maryam Montague
(page 102)
www.mymarrakesh.com
www.peacockpavilions.com

Jaime Mormann-
Richardson
(page 98)
www.sophistimom.com
www.jaimemormannphotography.com

Jennifer O'Connor
(page 116)
www.EarthAngelsToys.com
www.EarthAngelsToys.blogspot.com

Fifi O'Neill
(page 122)
www.fabulousfifi.typepad.com
coconut19@verizon.net

Béatrice Peltre
(page 130)
www.latartinegourmande.com
www.beatricepeltre.com
bea@latartinegourmande.com

Beth Price
(page 136)
www.leitesculinaria.com
beth@leitesculinaria.com

Jael Rattigan
(page 142)
www.frenchbroadchocolates.com

Celeste Shaw
(page 148)
www.chapsgirl.com
mychaps@msn.com

Serena Thompson
(page 154)
www.thefarmchicks.com
www.thefarmchicks.typepad.com

Molly Wizenberg
(page 160)
www.orangette.blogspot.com
www.delanceyseattle.com

Dana Wootton
(page 168)
www.danatreat.com
danatreat@gmail.com

More to Celebrate
Nope! We didn't overlook those fabulous
dishes these talented women "dished"
about in their stories … our plate was full
and we just didn't have room to squeeze in
one more recipe; but when there is a will,
there is a way. Any dish you may have seen
(and salivated over!) whose recipe could
not be found, just click on our website,
www.wherewomencook.com,
and you will find it there. Bon appétit!

conversions & equivalents

Metric Conversion Chart by Volume
(for Liquids)

U.S.	Metric (milliliters/liters)
¼ teaspoon	1.25 mL
½ teaspoon	2.5 mL
1 teaspoon	5 mL
1 tablespoon	15 mL
¼ cup	60 mL
½ cup	120 mL
¾ cup	180 mL
1 cup	240 mL
2 cups (1 pint)	480 mL
4 cups (1 quart)	960 mL
4 quarts (1 gallon)	3.8 L

Metric Conversion Chart by Weight
(for Dry Ingredients)

U.S.	Metric (grams/kilograms)
¼ teaspoon	1 g
½ teaspoon	2 g
1 teaspoon	5 g
1 tablespoon	15 g
16 ounces (1 pound)	450 g
2 pounds	900 g
3 pounds	1.4 kg
4 pounds	1.8 kg
5 pounds	2.3 kg
6 pounds	2.7 kg

Temperature Conversion

Fahrenheit	Celsius
32°	0°
212°	100°
250°	121°
275°	135°
300°	149°
350°	177°
375°	191°
400°	204°
425°	218°

Cooking Measurement Equivalents

3 teaspoons = 1 tablespoon

2 tablespoons = 1 fluid ounce

4 tablespoons = ¼ cup

5 tablespoons + 1 teaspoon = ⅓ cup

8 tablespoons = ½ cup

10 tablespoons + 2 teaspoons = ⅔ cup

12 tablespoons = ¾ cup

16 tablespoons = 1 cup

48 teaspoons = 1 cup

1 cup = 8 fluid ounces

2 cups = 1 pint

2 pints = 1 quart

4 quarts = 1 gallon

73

index

party's over